Islam and Open Society

Islam and Open Society

Fidelity and Movement in the Philosophy of Muhammad Iqbal

Souleymane Bachir Diagne

Translated from French to English by
Melissa McMahon

CODESRIA

Council for the Development of Social Science Research in Africa
DAKAR

© CODESRIA 2010

First published in French as « Islam et société ouverte : la fidélité et le mouvement dans la pensée de Muhammad Iqbal », Paris : Maisonneuve & Larose

Council for the Development of Social Science Research in Africa,

Avenue Cheikh Anta Diop, Angle Canal IV, BP 3304 Dakar, 18524, Senegal

Website: www.codesria.org

ISBN: 978-2-86978-305-8

Layout: Hadijatou Sy

Cover Design: Ibrahima Fofana

Printed by: Imprimerie Graphi plus, Dakar, Senegal

Distributed in Africa by CODESRIA

Distributed elsewhere by African Books Collective, Oxford, UK.

Website: www.africanbookscollective.com

The Council for the Development of Social Science Research in Africa (CODESRIA) is an independent organisation whose principal objectives are to facilitate research, promote research-based publishing and create multiple forums geared towards the exchange of views and information among African researchers. All these are aimed at reducing the fragmentation of research in the continent through the creation of thematic research networks that cut across linguistic and regional boundaries.

CODESRIA publishes a quarterly journal, *Africa Development*, the longest standing Africa-based social science journal; *Afrika Zamani*, a journal of history; the *African Sociological Review*; the *African Journal of International Affairs*; *Africa Review of Books* and the *Journal of Higher Education in Africa*. The Council also co-publishes the *Africa Media Review*; *Identity, Culture and Politics: An Afro-Asian Dialogue*; *The African Anthropologist* and the *Afro-Arab Selections for Social Sciences*. The results of its research and other activities are also disseminated through its Working Paper Series, Green Book Series, Monograph Series, Book Series, Policy Briefs and the *CODESRIA Bulletin*. Select CODESRIA publications are also accessible online at www.codesria.org.

CODESRIA would like to express its gratitude to the Swedish International Development Cooperation Agency (SIDA/SAREC), the International Development Research Centre (IDRC), the Ford Foundation, the MacArthur Foundation, the Carnegie Corporation, the Norwegian Agency for Development Cooperation (NORAD), the Danish Agency for International Development (DANIDA), the French Ministry of Cooperation, the United Nations Development Programme (UNDP), the Netherlands Ministry of Foreign Affairs, the Rockefeller Foundation, FINIDA, the Canadian International Development Agency (CIDA), the Open Society Initiative for West Africa (OSIWA), TrustAfrica, UN/UNICEF, the African Capacity Building Foundation (ACBF) and the Government of Senegal for supporting its research, training and publication programmes.

To my mother

To seek our points of departure by freely immersing ourselves in the problems themselves and in the demands that are coextensive with them.

Edmund Husserl

Contents

Acknowledgements

My father, Sheikh Diagne Ahmadou, introduced me to Muhammad Iqbal; he was also the first attentive reader of this work, inspired by his teaching of an Islam conceived in accordance with what Iqbal calls here 'The spirit of the caliph Umar'. My friends – Maziar Djoneidi, Catherine Clément, Philippe Gouet and Sémou Pathé Guèye – have given me the benefit of their comments. My thanks also go to all those with whom I discussed this essay during my period at Northwestern University, Charles Taylor and Dilip Parameshwar Gaonkar in particular. I have not forgotten those who attended the seminar I devoted to 'Muhammad Iqbal's philosophy of action' at the Cheikh Anta Diop University in Dakar between 1997 and 1999. Papa Amadou Ndiaye Bombé was one of them and he already knew, before leaving this world, how to think with Iqbal.

Preface

We must reread Iqbal. For a time we could imagine him forgotten, consigned to the oubliettes with the other figures of Islamic 'modernism' from the beginning of this century. But he had to come back.

There are effectively some transient 'modernisms' which try to adapt a secular tradition to the fashion of the day. They create themselves within an immediate present, which they then find it hard to survive. There are others which start with a major detour, a return to sources, in order to discover how to be truly faithful to them in a novel historical situation.

Iqbal's thought is of this second character, a rare and powerful realisation of the genre in fact. Along his millenarian journey, he manages to establish a mutual and fruitful exchange between thinkers and texts that are quite distant from each other: Nietzsche and Bergson, Hallaj and Rûmi, and between those and still others, taken up in the context of rereading the Quran.

So we still need to read Iqbal, each in his or her own way. Those of us for example – yesterday readers of Bergson, today of Heidegger – who are looking for an understanding of lived time, of historicity, beyond the objective, spatialized fixation of cosmic time, would find it worthwhile to reconsider all of that in the light of Iqbal's reinterpretation of the Quranic conception of 'destiny'. And similarly, we readers of Nietzsche would benefit from the Iqbalian understanding of the overman, coming on the heels of the 'perfect man' of the Sufi tradition.

Such ideas are current preoccupations in the contemporary West. But we also have shared reasons, Western, Muslim and Eastern merged together, in reading this remarkable man. Because our dialogues are troubled by a deep and mutual distrust. This distrust is partly derived from our own uncertainty regarding our identity, which sometimes gives us a feeling of insecurity under the gaze of others. It's this feeling that can lead to a sort of hyper-confidence, tightening around a rigid identity, and the belligerent rejection of the other as the bearer of evil. To seek out and define oneself using references found in the other's tradition becomes impossible, becomes treasonous.

But we all need to redefine ourselves, and we have a great deal to learn from one another in this search for a renewed self. This is why our current situation of frozen and distrustful relations is catastrophic for everyone.

In this atmosphere of suspicion and anger, it is a joy to hear the voice of Iqbal, both passionate and serene. It is the voice of a soul that is deeply anchored in the Quranic Revelation, and precisely for that reason, open to all the other voices, seeking in them the path of his own fidelity. It is the voice of a man who has left behind all identitarian rigidity, who has 'broken all the idols of tribe and caste' to address himself to all human beings. But an unhappy accident has meant that this voice was buried, both in the general forgetting of Islamic modernism and in the very country that he named before its existence Pakistan, whose multiple rigidities – political, religious, military – constitute a continual refutation of the very essence of his thought.

But we all need to hear him again, citizens of the West, Muslims, and those from his native India, where a form of Hindu chauvinism rages in our times that exceeds his worst fears. Souleymane Bachir Diagne has done all of us an immense favor in making this voice once again clear and convincing.

This small book has pulled off the gargantuan task of presenting Iqbal's thought in all of its actuality, by making us feel once again the constitutive tensions that this thought sought to resolve: between the affirmation of man and openness to God, between fidelity and movement, between the falsafa and the sense of the real, between universalism and belonging. Better still, by reclaiming this thought within the context of today's concerns, Bachir continues the movement that is essential to the Iqbalian approach; he brings together voices that are quite far apart in time and place, to the place where they can once again speak to each other. And this is of great benefit, as they have a lot to say to each other. We are all deeply grateful to him for it.

Charles Taylor
Professor at McGill University
Quebec, Canada

Introduction

Referring to his major philosophical work, *The Reconstruction of Religious Thought in Islam*, Muhammad Iqbal (1877–1938) confided to one of his colleagues that if his book had been written during the reign of the Abbasid caliph Al-Ma'mun – from 813 to 832 – it would have had profound repercussions in all of the Islamic intellectual world. Simply, an author's pride or even arrogance? To evaluate this judgement, and in the first place to properly understand it, we must recall the nature of the reign of the caliph Al-Ma'mun and what it meant, in particular, for the emergence and development of philosophical thought in Islamic civilisation.

The name Al-Ma'mun is associated with the House of Wisdom (*bayt al hikma*), an institute he created in the year 832, in Baghdad, the capital of the Abbassids, to accommodate the scholars who had the task of translating into Arabic the different Greek sciences – the mathematics of Euclid and Archimedes, the logic and physics of Aristotle, etc.: in short, philosophy and the disciplines it envelops.

We can consider this foundation of the House of Wisdom to mark a beginning in relation to the tradition of thought that was to emerge from the encounter between Greek and Hellenistic philosophy on the one hand, and on the other the spiritual universe of Islam: that which came to be known under the Arabized Greek name of *falsafa*. And whose consequence was the creation of a new class of scholars: the *falâsifa* (singular: *faylasûf*).

It didn't go without saying, when one was the 'Commander of the faithful', to even admit the idea of a 'wisdom' that could come from those – the Greeks – who were, after all, only pagans! Legend has dramatized this reticence, this resistance even faced with a thought that was foreign to the universe of the Revelation in the form of a dream of the Caliph. He saw in a dream, it is said, the philosopher Aristotle himself who had come especially to reassure him and to assure him that ultimately there was barely any contradiction between religion and philosophy, and that the latter could be useful for understanding the former better. Such a divine sign was certainly needed to justify the foundation of an institution dedicated to 'wisdom' that was positioned outside the traditional religious sciences.

There was a great tension between two possible attitudes. On the one hand the attitude that would have consisted in saying that all wisdom was contained within the religious sciences organically linked to the Revelation: books that said the same thing would be superfluous then, and those that said something different would be potentially dangerous. On the other hand, the attitude of openness and acceptance of the movement, which had for its own part at least two prophetic traditions: the tradition that commanded Muslims to go in search of knowledge/science, be it in China; another – which precisely drew on the concept of 'wisdom' – that declares that this wisdom is a 'lost property' of the Muslim, who then has the right to consider himself more entitled to it than anyone else, wherever he may find it.

It is because the reign of the caliph Al-Ma'mun represented the victory of openness and movement, and because the House of Wisdom marked – symbolically – the birth of a spirit of free research and concern for the truth that Muhammad Iqbal wanted to place his philosophical work, over a millennia later, under its aegis so to speak.

We must also add that this evocation of the time of Al-Ma'mun and its 'philosophical' action is normal for the reformist Islamic thinkers of the nineteenth century, within the so-called modernist thought of the new Islamic philosophers. Not in the sense of a nostalgic evocation of a Golden Age, but as the expression of a possibility, always still to be realised, of a restless and questioning – open – thought. We thus find very often in the writings of Sayyid Amir Ali (1849–1929), who was the first in British India to create an Indo-Islamic political organ, the National Muhammadan Association, the idea that the true spirit of Islam was fully expressed during what was the period of emergence of the ideas of rationalist theology of the Mu'tazilite school, which inspired the actions of the caliph. Considering that Al-Ma'mun was for the Islamic world what Augustus was for Rome or Pericles for Athens, Amir Ali pays homage to this school whose expansion was encouraged by the caliph in these terms:

> Mu'tazilaism, is unquestionably the most rationalistic and liberal phase of Islâm. In its liberalism, in its sympathy with all phases of human thought, its grand hopefulness and expansiveness, it represents the ideas of the philosophers of the House of Mohammed who reflected the thoughts of the Master.[1]

And when it is a question, for example, of reflecting on the status of women and of discovering within the very movement deployed by the principles of Islam, what for current times would represent a clear insight into what religion says on this matter; it is to a reading of Mu'tazilism that he returns to conclude his lesson with, 'The Mu'tazila is, by conviction, a strict monogamist.'[2]

It is by inscribing his thought within modern and contemporary philosophy from Descartes to Bergson, and by making it face the scientific revolutions – relativity, quantum mechanics… – that had overthrown the categories of time, space and causality, that Muhammad Iqbal, this *faylasûf* of today, renewed for our own era the approach that had been at the very foundation of the House of Wisdom. The 'profound repercussions' that he could have expected in response to his thought, in the time and conditions that gave birth to the *falsafa*, are simply the resumption of this movement, the renaissance of the spirit of restlessness, whose necessity so current at the end of the nineteenth century, makes itself felt acutely.

Primarily, what we know about Muhammad Iqbal, is that he was one of the main inspirations behind the idea of an independent Pakistan. As such, he occupies in this country the position of a 'founding father' so to speak. But his thought certainly goes a great deal beyond the framework within which it emerged – that of the struggle against colonialism for the freedom of India as well as the violent clash between Hindu and Islamic nationalisms that led to the rupture we know of today. The philosophical oeuvre written by Muhammad Iqbal is particularly enlightening, and useful today, because we have reason to reflect on the conditions of modernity in Islamic societies confronted with the necessity – that his thought helps to convert into a task – of renewing its acquaintance with the spirit of permanent reform and openness as well as with the values that express this spirit: the affirmation of the individual, the value accorded to judgement unencumbered by the weight of tradition, the scientific spirit, the idea of progress, freedom….

Chapter I

A *faylasûf* of Today

At the end of his poem translated into English under the title *The Mysteries of Selflessness*,[3] Muhammad Iqbal addresses a prayer to God entrusting Him with the posterity of his work. Thus, the same author who in the Prologue of another of his long philosophical poems entitled *The Secrets of the Self*, had declared that his message, bearer of 'things that are yet unborn in the world',[4] was addressed to the future – *I have no need of the ear of To-day, I am the voice of the poet of To-morrow*[5] – came to wish that his thought, if it came to represent a thought 'astray' and 'thorns' dangerous to those coming across it, should be in this case 'choked' and deprived of growth as an 'untimely seed'. On the other hand, he implores, if it has reflected something of the truth, may the 'April shower' turn into 'pearls of great and glittering price'.[6]

We must no doubt imagine that the mirror was not without 'luster', to borrow his words, since the author presented by Eva de Vitray-Meyerovitch as the greatest poet and most important philosopher of our era from the Indian sub-continent, translated into several languages, has become the 'intellectual model for several tens of millions of men'.[7]

Muhammad Iqbal was born 9 November 1877[8] in the Punjab city of Sialkot. It was his grandfather, Sheikh Rafiq, who came to settle in this town along with his three brothers, in 1857, following the example of numerous Kashmiri Muslims pushed into exile in the Punjab province by the political situation in this region. The biographies indicate that his father, a tailor by trade, was in a position to raise his children in a Sufi Islamic tradition, while supporting the full cost of a modern education, which he did not have himself, was able to direct his children on the path of brilliant scholarship.

Thus Iqbal's older brother, Ata Muhammad (1860–1940), undertook a career as an engineer while his younger brother was more of a literary type who was deeply affected, at Murray College[9] in his native city, by the teaching of Maulvî Sayyid Mîr Hasan (1844–1929), an instructor particularly well versed in Arabic and Persian writings.[10] At the end of these first years of education, he held for several years a teaching position in philosophy at the Government College in Lahore before instigating a decisive phase in his life by going to Europe to pursue tertiary studies.

His friend, Abdul Qadir, explains[11] that his own travel to Europe encouraged Iqbal to join him there after obtaining the financial support for the expenses involved from his older brother. Regarding the three-year period spent by Iqbal in England, from 1905 to 1908, Abdul Qadir declares that they represented a crucial time in his personal story and in that of his work.[12] In Great Britain, he encountered the schoolmaster Sir Thomas W. Arnold (1864-1930), the philosopher and orientalist who had been his teacher and his friend at Government College in Lahore where he taught from 1898 to 1904 before returning to London. Thus one year before Iqbal was to join him there: the Urdu poem that his departure from India inspired in his disciple is an expression of the desire Arnold transmitted to him to push, ever further, his quest for knowledge.[13]

At Cambridge, in parallel with his philosophical studies, Muhammad Iqbal received a training and a degree in law, which opened up the career he embraced on his return to his country. Notably, in 1907, he prepared a thesis entitled *The Development of Metaphysics in Persia* with, as its subtitle, *A Contribution to the History of Muslim Philosophy*.[14] To the degree obtained from Cambridge, he was to add a doctorate from the University of Munich: after having spent several months in Germany and having acquired a certain knowledge of German, he presented there a version of his thesis in this language. This thesis, published in 1908, in London, with a dedication to his teacher Arnold, who he thanked for ten years of training in philosophy, immediately attracted a great deal of attention.

As we have seen, Muhammad Iqbal had already written an abundant body of poetry in Urdu. His son, Javid Iqbal, was to say of this poetry that it belonged to his 'research period', which he places between 1895 and 1912. During this time, he notes, his father wrote *ghazals* in imitation of the 'Dagh conventional style', as well as poems exalting Indian nationalism in general; to which must also be added the poems for children that resemble 'Urdu adaptations of Emerson, William Cowper, Longfellow or even Tennyson'.[15] Of all the poems of this first period – which were published in 1924 – the most moving, writes Javid Iqbal, are those that express the cry of Muslims engaged in India or the Middle-East, in the fight for their independence.[16] In a general sense, he considers these first poems as a testament to what may have been Iqbal's state of mind at the time he went to Europe; a state of mind that can be summed up by a few convictions: nationalism, faith in Islamic solidarity and a certain Sufi pantheism. Muhammad Iqbal will later consider this period, as his son goes on to report, as belonging to 'his phase of ignorance and madness'.[17]

The poet's stay in Europe subsequently led him to a new phase in which he adopted for his poetry, which 'thus attains a prophetic quality', the Persian language – 'the language of Islamic culture' – instead of Urdu, as 'the message was henceforth addressed to Muslims worldwide'.[18] This message first took the form of the poem titled *The Secrets of the Self*, the first instalment, in 1915, of a poetico-philosophical trilogy in Persian, whose second instalment was *The Mysteries of Selflessness*, published three years later and the third *The Message from the East*.

This new phase will also be that of the active and more direct role Iqbal took in the political upheavals India was undergoing. As a result, in 1926, he is elected as a member of the Punjab Legislative Council. In 1930, he is appointed President of the annual meeting of the Islamic League. It is at this time that the philosopher, whose whole thought nevertheless indicates that he refuses with his whole being 'these idols represented by race or nationality'[19] declares himself clearly in favour of an autonomous Islamic state, thus becoming from the perspective of history, even if he did not see it realised before his death in 1938, one of the founders, if not *the* founder, of the idea of Pakistan.

Javid Iqbal, remarking on the mysterious connection that, according to him, has always existed between great problems and great poems like *The Divine Comedy*, *Paradise Lost*, *Faust* or *Mathnavi*, writes, 'in its highest form, poetry is more philosophical than philosophy itself'.[20] Later on, the *Lectures* given by Iqbal during a tour, in 1928–29, of southern India, at the invitation of the Muslim Association of Madras, when they were later published in English by their author, under the title *Lectures on the Reconstruction of Religious Thought in Islam* in 1930, gave philosophical expression to his thought in prose.[21] But it is also, and perhaps especially in the highest form of poetry that this *reconstruction* will be carried out, on the foundation of the affirmation of the self via the ego, after this latter is truly constituted as the result of what could be called, with Gaston Berger, 'the walk towards the *I*'.

Chapter II

A Philosophy of the Individual

One of the most well-known Islamic mystics, Hussein ibn Mansur al-Hallaj, was beheaded in Baghdad in 922 for having declared, in a famous theopathic utterance: *ana'l Haqq*, which is to say, as Louis Massignon translates, 'I am the creating Truth = my 'I' is God'.[22]

But which 'I' is speaking in the man who says '*I* am the Truth'? It should be truth itself, so inconceivable is it that such a predicate could be attributed to a finite ego. Truth alone being able, truthfully, to testify for itself, only an 'I' previously annulled by it, and in it, could, not *profess regarding itself* 'I am the Truth', but be the *instrument* of this testimony. Only in such a way can the very act of positing oneself as a witness not change the unicity, the 'aloneness' of what it bears witness to.

When this unicity that leaves nothing outside of it is fully realised, to say 'I am the Truth', like a drop of water saying 'I am the Ocean', is not to make a scandalous statement but simply to recognise the impossibility of being fully oneself, of being able to claim a separate position in one's finiteness in order to speak to the infinite in the accusative and say to it: '*you* are the truth'. This utterance thus appears as the sign of an absorption of the 'I' into the totality, and its ultimate meaning would be the same as an indefinite repetition of the third person: '*Him*'...

Muhammad Iqbal invites us to transform our perspective, to turn aside from this path of absorption, and the metaphysics it expresses, to one of 'the loving embrace of the finite': 'In the higher Sufism of Islam', he writes, 'unitive experience is not the finite ego effacing its own identity by some sort of absorption into the Infinite Ego; it is rather the Infinite passing into the loving embrace of the finite'.[23] He thus invites us to turn our back on a Sufism of extinction for a philosophy of action founded, on the contrary, on a self-affirmation that is more faithful, according to him, to what represents the true Quranic conception both of 'the value and destiny of the human ego'.[24]

Self-affirmation

In his presentation of *The Development of Metaphysics in Persia*, Muhammad Iqbal draws on the metaphysics of Sufism, and on the notion, which is an essential feature of this metaphysics, of the 'impersonal absorption' which he says appears for the first time in Bayazid Bistami; and as a consequence of such a notion, he explains that we will inevitably be led to the famous and 'hopelessly pantheistic' *logion* of Hussein ibn Mansur al-Hallaj 'who, following the true spirit of Indian Vedantism, exclaimed: 'I am God' (*Aham Brahma asmi*)'.[25]

This is a case of the condensed expression of a pantheistic metaphysics which, turning its back on an emanative and neo-Platonic theory of creation,[26] will conceive it rather as being, in a passive mode so to speak, the reflected image of eternal Beauty. An image reflected in nature and equally in human being, who would thus be wrong to think of themselves as entities apart: all sense of separation according to such a doctrine would simply be the result of ignorance of this essential truth that alterity is mere appearance, a dream, a shadow that could never, when faced with the sole Reality, achieve the consistency of an 'I' or mark the emergence, in the heart of Being, of *personality*.

A necessary consequence that follows such a set of premises is that immortality is always impersonal. In the terms of an Aristotelian such as Ibn Rushd (Averroès), for example, immortality only properly belongs to the universal active Intellect alone; who is, in effect, *no one*. And such an immortality would have no other significance then than being the final reabsorption of the false multiplicity of shadows into the light of the impersonal totality.

> Intelligence, according to Ibn-i-Rushd', writes Iqbal: 'is not from of the body; it belongs to a different order of being, and transcends individuality. It is, therefore, one, universal, and eternal. This obviously means that, since unitary intellect transcends individuality, its appearance as so many unities in the multiplicity of human persons, is a mere illusion. The eternal unity of intellect may mean, as Renan thinks, the everlastingness of humanity and civilization; it does not surely mean personal immortality.[27]

The metaphysical alternative is thus between a monism of Being from which no 'creation' would be able to emerge from Himself or ontological pluralism. 'Thus it is' Iqbal says 'that monist and pluralist thought have responded to each other dialectically throughout history, taking different forms each time according to the context'. And we can see 'he adds' in the way the pluralism of beings, that Leibniz called monads, represented an objection to the pantheism of Spinoza which followed from his definition of substance as being, in all necessity, singular, an analogy to the path taken by Wâhid Mahmûd who, in the 8th century, opposed the monistic doctrines and taught that 'reality is not one, but many – primary living units which combine in various ways, and gradually rise to perfection by passing through an ascending scale of forms'.[28]

The universe, Wahîd Mahmûd also says, still explaining his metaphysical atomism, is composed of *afrâd*, 'essential units, or simple atoms which have existed from all eternity, and are endowed with life. The law of the Universe is an ascending perfection of elemental matter, continually passing from lower to higher forms determined by the kind of food which the fundamental units assimilate'.[29]

The Iqbalian philosophy of the affirmation of the consistency of the individual self will be able to reconnect with the principle of this pluralist reaction to monism, in the same way that it will retain the idea, such as it is found in Suhrawardî's philosophy of *Illumination*, of a continuous movement which is the spiritual progress of individual souls that is not ended even by death: 'The individual souls, after death, are not unified into one Soul, but continue different from each other in proportion to the *illumination* they received during their companionship with physical organisms'.[30]

The amount of *illumination* received qualifies individuals differently. Two souls cannot be the same, which would then justify their ultimate reabsorption into the heart of the one undifferentiated totality that would be identical to them. On the contrary, for Suhrawardî, who Iqbal states that he anticipated the Leibnizian theory of indiscernables,[31] the continuous journey of souls traces differentiated and individualized spiritual trajectories. This progress is always the state of a soul-body unity welded together by love and occupied by the desire for *illumination* and it's this unity that is the site of the human ideal of ascension in the scale of being, which also constitutes a continuous process of emerging freedom, which is to say awareness of self as being a distinct individuality:[32] awareness of self as *personality*.

Overall, even if we can see pantheistic aspects in Suhrawardî's illuminationist philosophy, it remains, for Iqbal, that it posits two affirmations that will be close to the principle of his own thought: *the world is something real and the human soul is a distinct individuality*. In virtue of these affirmations, the illuminationist philosophy breaks with the metaphysics of a certain Sufism of the extinction of individuality in the Whole. This is the same break that Muhammad Iqbal's philosophy of self and action will make, where it is a matter, as he writes at the end of his *Development of Metaphysics in Persia* of turning away from 'pure speculation and dreamy mysticism' to 'rouse the spirit to a consciousness of the stern reality of things'.[33]

The Test of Consistency

The ultimate end of the human ego is not to be absorbed in contemplation; it is not to *see* something, Iqbal declares, following on in the words that conclude his *Lectures* and where he discloses the ego's moment of 'supreme bliss' as well as its 'greatest trial' at the same time: 'It is in the ego's effort to *be* something that he discovers his final opportunity to sharpen his objectivity and acquire a more fundamental 'I am' which finds evidence of its reality not in the Cartesian 'I think' but in the Kantian 'I can'. The end of the ego's quest is not emancipation from the limitations of individuality; it is, on the other hand, a more precise definition of it. The final act is not an intellectual act, but a vital act which deepens the whole being of the ego, and sharpens his will with the creative assurance that the world is not merely something to be seen and known through concepts, but something to be made and re-made through continuous action. It is a moment of supreme bliss and also a moment of the greatest trial for the ego...'[34]

This passage perfectly illuminates the notion that is at the heart of Iqbalian thought, that of *khudî*, the self, which, far from pursuing its own annihilation within the light of the Whole, affirms itself on the contrary, before God Himself. The desire to bear witness to one's own being – simply because to be is precisely to show oneself as a desire to be – is not extinguished in the divine Presence. Or rather, this desire to be needs, at its finest extremity, to have God Himself as its witness and its test, so to speak. In the language of poetry, as found in the *Book of Eternity*, this witnessing by God of the finite ego is evoked as follows:

> Invoke the aid of three witnesses to verify thy 'Station'.
> The first witness is thine own consciousness –
> See thyself, then, with thine own light.
> The second witness is the consciousness of another ego –
> See thyself, then, with the light of an ego other than thee.
> The third witness is God's consciousness –
> See thyself, then, with God's light.
> If thou standest unshaken in front of this light,
> Consider thyself as living and eternal as He!
> That man alone is real who dares –
> Dares to see God face to face! [35]

This theme of individual reality that is experienced even at the level of divine Reality is present everywhere in Iqbal's poetic work. It is, he indicates, the significance of the attitude, given as an example, of the Prophet of Islam when, faced with ultimate Reality: 'the eye did not waver, nor yet did it stray' (Quran 53:17), and it forms the motif of some of the strongest images in his poetry: that, for example, of the atom that feels its own light in the presence of the sun, that of the drop of water that persists even in the depths of the ocean...

It is a theme that is organically connected to another that also pervades Iqbal's poetic work and which concerns the consistency, the solidity of the ego. Thus, the drop of water persists precisely because it has been able to take on the consistency of the pearl; the wave retains its being because it is sculpted by its movement; if coal and the diamond have the same origins, the diamond is what it is because in its ripened and solidified form it has taken on its own hardness, whereas: 'When the mountain loses its self, it turns into sands'.[36]

We can observe the metaphysical reversal that Muhammad Iqbal performs in the significance he henceforth gives to mystical experience according to this perspective of self-affirmation. The Hallajian experience in particular comes to be thought in a totally different way to what it seemed to mean when it was evoked in *The Development of Metaphysics in Persia*; and from now on the Sufi martyr is given, when the poet encounters him in 'The Sphere of Jupiter', the task of speaking against the negation represented by the annihilation of self: 'You who seek your goal in annihilation', 'non-existence can never discover existence'.[37]

We are indebted to the work of Louis Massignon, who collected and published the *Fragments d'Halladj* and thus allowed us to have a more faithful perspective on the meaning of his famous words, to have understood in this way the true interpretation of his experience. Consequently, Iqbal writes, we can understand that this 'is not the drop slipping into the sea, but the realisation and bold affirmation in an undying phrase of the reality of the human ego in a profounder personality'.[38]

From this perspective, there is no comparison with the destiny of the Fallen Angel, Satan, which cannot be read as a 'personalist testimony', according to a reading which is effectively encountered within the Sufi tradition, where it is a matter of taking the full measure of the ambivalence of the rebellion of one who was initially a prince among angels. Satan is in effect that being who learned to say 'I', and, thus discovering ego and personality, ultimately exiled himself within the pathology of self that is egoism: 'Thy soul cares only for itself, like the camel: 'It is self-conceited, self-governed, and self-willed'.[39]

It remains nonetheless that he stood in this way against the order to bow before a creature, keeping in mind the 'only venerable prostration': 'The only venerable prostration, Is the one that excludes all others'!'[40]

In this sense, his revolt carries the positive message of self-affirmation as witness to Unity and that of a negation which went on to make the self a self formed by jealousy, a self that ends up expressing nothing more than resentment: 'I am better than he: Thou hast created me out of fire, whereas him Thou hast created out of clay' (Quran 38:76), Satan says to explain his refusal to prostrate himself before him who God has nevertheless 'breathed into him of His spirit' (Quran 15:29).

The stance of the 'divine rebel' carries for man – for he has to learn what he must become – a lesson that is expressed through the complaint Satan addresses to God, in the *Javid Nama*, bitterly regretting not having in humanity an adversary worthy of him, precisely because humanity has not known how to acquire the consistency and solidity of an 'I' and doesn't have the personality, hard like a diamond, to oppose to the fire he himself has been created from:

> This runt Adam, what is he? A handful of twigs; and all a handful of twigs needs is a spark coming from me. If all that exists in this world is twigs, what is the use of having given me so much fire? It is not much to melt glass, but to melt stone counts for something! ... I want a creature who turns my head, whose gaze makes me tremble. A man who would say to me: 'Get out of my sight.' A man before whom I would no longer be worth anything. Oh God! A living man who loves the truth! Perhaps then I would take pleasure in defeat![41]

The aim is thus to become a person and this happens through action. It is in action that the conquest of personality occurs, that the 'I' emerges and acquires more and more consistency; it is also in action that it is tested. Like the 'restless wave', the 'I' becomes aware of itself not in an 'I am' of the pure reflexive grasp of oneself, but an 'I am' that is revealed to oneself by being revealed in action.

In a poem whose title is precisely *Action and Life*, in the collection *Message from the East*,[42] the wave says: 'To roll on is to be, to lie still not to be'. The heart of the Iqbalian philosophy is this movement, this permanent restlessness that is life itself, for always: 'Life seeks to build a new universe'.[43] It's thus in this way that we must think the universe as the permanent project, the always-open construction site of the ultimate ego, continuously creative, from which the other egos proceed. Not then like a world emerging ready-made from an instantaneous act of creation achieved once and for all, a world that henceforth only offers itself for contemplation, a world to be *seen*, but, on the contrary, as a world to *be* and consequently, to act, a world for *becoming-person*.

A Cosmology of Emergence

The stakes of a philosophy of the self is not simply saving the finite ego from impersonality. It is also, and perhaps firstly, ultimate Reality that it is a case of offering to be thought as being genuinely an ego. It is the very conception of God that it is a matter of releasing, as well, from a pantheism that would make of Him 'some vague, vast and pervasive cosmic element, such as light', as Iqbal states in the third of his *Lectures* devoted to 'The Conception of God and the Meaning of Prayer'.[44]

Dwelling on this last comparison of God with light, which he reminds us is encountered in the three monotheistic religions of Judaism, Christianity and Islam, the poet-philosopher indicates that the well-known verse in the Quran (24:35) that identifies God with 'the light of the Heavens and of the earth', seems on the contrary to invite us to conceive of an individual using this metaphor. Let us consider the verse in its totality, which is to say what Iqbal calls the 'development of the metaphor': 'His light is like a niche in which is a lamp – the lamp encased in glass – the glass, as it were, a star'.

This description, he says, 'is meant rather to exclude the suggestion of a formless cosmic element by centralizing the light in a flame which is further individualized by its encasement in glass likened unto a well-defined star'.[45]

Generally speaking, the concept of God as an individual is central in the Quranic notion of God whose ultimate expression is Iqbal says. This *sura* is given as the very definition of divinity and which is thus called, for this reason the *sura* of 'pure faith' or of 'deep religion' according to Jacques Berque's translation. The verse is as follows:

> SAY: 'He is the One God:
> God the Eternal, the Uncaused Cause of All Being.
> He begets not, and neither is He begotten;
> and there is nothing that could be compared with Him'.[46]

To hear these lines is to understand that they indicate to us the very significance of individuality. On this point, Iqbal says, there is an important lesson to draw from the thought of Henri Bergson concerning individuality or, more precisely, what he calls the tendency to individuation: 'while the tendency to individuate is everywhere present in the organized world, it is everywhere opposed by the tendency towards reproduction. For the individuality to be perfect, it would be necessary that no detached part of the organism could live separately. But then reproduction would be impossible. For what is reproduction, but the building up of a new organism with a detached fragment of the old? Individuality therefore harbours its enemy at home'.[47]

Muhammad Iqbal, who quotes this passage, deduces from it that at the summit of the scale that constitutes beings according to the degree to which what we may call a 'becoming-individual' has been achieved within them, the accomplished individual can only think itself as one in which there is absolutely no trace of the 'enemy' tendency to leave oneself. Because it is perfect, this individual is necessarily then 'closed off as an ego, peerless and unique'.[48] It is not, however, totally closed in on itself, after the mode of the divine in Aristotle – which Aristotle defines as a 'thought of his thought' to express that its nature consists entirely of immobile contemplation of its own eternity. Quite to the contrary – and here we can usefully elucidate Iqbal's suggestion by evoking the distinction made by Gaston Berger in his reading of Louis Lavelle's work and in particular what Lavelle says regarding Being: because it is perfect, the Individual is 'something else entirely than a static reality: it is an Act even if this is only an *action* that takes place within time'.[49]

This distinction between 'act' and 'action' is important because it is precisely a matter of avoiding what Aristotle himself sought to avoid by completely separating the divine from becoming: making it a prisoner of time by inscribing its activity within the succession of causes and effects. Furthermore, Iqbal indicates, this Aristotelian conception aiming to save divinity from the order of succession has not been without influence on the theological approach of certain thinkers in Islam, such as Ibn-i-Hazm, for example.[50] In effect, this Islamic theologian from Andalusia, who died in 1064, had been led to wonder about the meaning to give to an attribute like 'living', when it is predicated of God, precisely through fear of thus seeing the divine live, with a life that, by definition, is change. The solution he found is the prudently literalist one that consists of indicating that the only reason for speaking of God as living is that he Himself speaks of Himself in that way in His Book; it is thus understood that aside from this purely scriptural reference, the life of being is the price to pay in order to affirm His perfection.

For Iqbal however, it is necessary to be able to say that life is of being because it is the same thing to be and to be alive. But also, in effect, to be living and to be in movement is the same thing. Being is not enclosed within a 'life' that only pertains to its mystery and whose only relation to life, which is essentially movement, is one of pure homonymy. Such an enclosure would not make Being perfect, but 'utter inaction, a motiveless, stagnant neutrality, an absolute nothing.'[51] No doubt we don't refer to its action but more precisely of its act. To speak of an act rather than an action is thus to establish here a clear distinction between two radically different conceptions of time. Between the time of succession of causes and effects, that the intellect spreads out and cuts up following the analytic mode that is proper to it, and time as 'living creative *moment*' wholly within a 'now' where the *past* – what the separating intelligence calls such – operates within a *present* in which *future* possibilities open up.[52]

Being is not concluded from the thought of its inert perfection but from the experience of its creative movement. This formula could summarize the reproach Iqbal makes to the different forms of metaphysical argument to 'prove' God. They begin, he considers, by always positing a radical duality between thought and being, digging 'an unbridgeable gulf between the ideal and the real' and then wishing to reach the infinite by a simple negation of the finite.[53] In the end, these different arguments for proving God by manufacturing the infinite from the finite share with Zeno's paradox the desire to manufacture movement from immobility.

It is on the contrary movement that must serve as the point of departure, and the experience we have of it, this being possible precisely because 'thought and intuition are organically related', for which reason 'thought is capable of reaching an immanent Infinite in whose self-unfolding movement the various finite concepts are merely moments'.[54] It can thus be observed: this Iqbalian thought, one of whose foundational ideas is that there is a relation to the infinite within us that constitutes us and that it is 'the presence of the total Infinite in the movement of knowledge that makes finite thinking possible', can be understood both in the light of Spinoza's philosophy as well as Bergson which it willingly draws on.

This conception of Iqbal's according to which thought – as the world and as time – is full, so to speak, of the infinite goes then against the rationalist dogmatism that is expressed in the scholastic arguments that are offered as proofs of the existence of God; but it also refutes the Kantian attitude which 'failed to see that thought, in the very act of knowledge, passes beyond its own finitude',[55] an attitude that is comparable to that of Abu Hamid Al-Ghazâlî (1058-1111), the philosopher *Algazel* of the Middle Ages, who considered that thought, because it was condemned to be enclosed within finitude, necessarily had to abolish itself to give way to mystical experience alone.

Ghazâlî is moreover the author of a work entitled *The Incoherence of the Philosophers*,[56] which is the full expression of the conflict between speculative theology and philosophy in Islam, where he attempts to discuss and refute twenty theses that he believes sums up the doctrine of those who imported Greek metaphysics into the heart of the Islamic spiritual universe. There is one particular question which constitutes a point on which, according to Ghazâlî, these philosophers can be considered to be, quite simply, heretics: that of the co-eternity of the world of matter with God. This point which forms the topic of the first of the twenty discussions that make up the work is presented by Ghazâlî in the following way:

> The philosophers consider that the world has never ceased to exist with God ..., to be His effect, to exist together with Him and not to be posterior to Him in time in the way that the effect coexists with the cause and the light with the sun.[57]

The Iqbalian cosmology of emergence transforms the question itself by firstly pointing out that it is a matter of misconceiving it as a static confrontation between the creator and his creation. The misconception on the one hand consists in positing the creative act of God as finite, on the other hand of giving it an external aspect that confronts Him as an other and on which He would act from outside. The Creator in this case simply beholds the spectacle of creation. However, because the act of God is itself infinite, eternal, the universe never ceases to be in 'organic relation to the life of its maker', it is nothing other than the 'free creative energy' which unfolds itself in our interpretations of it as space, time or matter.[58] And it's in an analogous way that Iqbal conceives, regarding the finite ego, the philosophical question, traditional since Descartes, of the union of the soul and the body. It is not a matter of constituting them as substances that are so radically different that their union becomes unthinkable other than under the form of metaphors, necessarily approximate, like that of the captain and his ship; nor of explaining that if they influence each other despite their absolute independence, it is because of a pre-established harmony that arranges it so that the modalities of the body have, in a parallel fashion from all perspectives, their equivalent following the modalities of the soul, and reciprocally, and Iqbal has in mind here the Leibnizian position on the question.[59]

Contrary to the very conception that begins by establishing a radical separation between soul and body so as to then wonder how their union can be conceived, the Iqbalian philosophy presents the soul as the emergence of consciousness from a higher order outside of the lower-order 'colony of egos' that constitutes matter.[60] Thus, what we call life and mind is a 'creative synthesis' which makes emerge the *event* of an 'unforeseeable and novel fact on its own plane of being, and cannot be explained mechanistically'.[61] The body can thus be seen as a 'system of acts' that 'repeat themselves' linked to the 'spontaneity' of mind, such that the body will precisely be conceived as 'accumulated action' which, as such, is not detachable from the soul whose 'habit' it represents.[62] And Iqbal draws an analogy with the relationship of God to creation by pointing out that nature as a 'structure of events' and 'systematic mode of behaviour' appears as 'organic to the ultimate Self' and as the 'habit' of God, following a Quranic expression.[63]

In all, the Iqbalian philosophy aims to go beyond the thought of a creation external to its creator and to posit the creative activity of the ultimate Ego as a continuous act in an eternal present that is only broken down by thought: and the philosopher-poet recalls in this regard[64] that when a disciple said in the presence of Ba Yazid of Bistam that 'There was a moment of time when God existed and nothing else existed beside Him', the master replied: 'It is just the same now as it was then.'

The ultimate Ego will be presented, without It being subject to becoming since it is faced with nothing outside of it, as the immanent Self which animates and supports the whole of a continuous creation, of a 'growing universe and not an already completed product which left the hand of its maker ages ago, and is now lying stretched in space as a dead mass of matter to which time does nothing, and consequently is nothing'.[65] His cosmology of emergence represents a major theme of Iqbal's poetic oeuvre.

Thus, after his *Prologue*, the poem *The Secrets of the Self* opens on a cosmogenesis where we see that the Self, whose potential sleeps in each atom and whose 'nature' is 'to manifest itself' – The form of existence is an effect of the Self, 'Whatsoever thou seest is a secret of the Self' – does so by expending itself with a measureless generosity which is simply the unfolding of its overabundance:

> For the sake of a single rose it destroys a hundred rose gardens
> And makes a hundred lamentation in quest of a single melody.
> For one sky it produces a hundred new moons,
> And for one word a hundred discourses.
> The excuse for this wastefulness and cruelty
> Is the shaping and perfecting of spiritual beauty.

The 'wastefulness' and 'cruelty' in question are nothing here but the very features of the creative force of which art carries the trace, they are the manifestation of that for which 'The spaciousness of Time is the arena' and to whose very essence it is to always overflow, in an inexhaustible superabundance.

Incompleteness is not imperfection, but on the contrary creative tension which riddles a universe that is always to be made – as 'He adds to His creation whatever He wills' (Quran, 35:1) – and God is not on board *within* evolution – it is to us, to our human way of seeing, that one of His signs appears as the alternation of day and night – since He *is* the evolution that, from His point of view, outside of any order of succession, in pure duration, 'means unfailing realisation of the infinite creative possibilities of His being which retains its wholeness throughout the entire process.'[66] It is for this reason that, at several points in his *Lectures*, Iqbal recalls the prophetic saying that identifies God with time (*dahr*): 'Do not speak ill of time, for time is God.'

And thus, when we hold the two points of view together, we understand that, according to the words of the poet Goethe, whom he cites:[67] 'All the straining, all the striving Is eternal peace in God'.

Nor is incompleteness a blind *élan vital* that no teleology can shed light on, as if: 'Its flames burned a hundred Abrahams', it is so that 'That the lamp of one Muhammad might be lighted'.[68]

And it is on this point that Muhammad Iqbal parts ways with Bergson – for whom, we learn from Louis Massignon, he immediately felt a spiritual affinity. In his *Lectures* he says that he is the only contemporary thinker to have engaged in philosophical reflection on the notion of duration.[69]

According to Bergson, 'when I look towards my conscious experience and ask myself what "existing" means to me, I encounter a series of successive states, feelings and representations that vary continually, and above all continuously, such that in all rigor I shouldn't even speak of a state, a word that precisely implies a certain *stability*'. Thus, Bergson says in the first pages of *Creative Evolution*, 'My mental state, as it advances on the road of time, is continually swelling with the duration which it accumulates: it goes on increasing – rolling upon itself, as a snowball on the snow'.[70] If we thus speak of a *state*, it is precisely because our attention manufactures a discontinuous psychological life, which distinguishes and separates, where there is the continuity of a flow, states which will then be joined up again, as one threads pearls, by a self who would be their immutable substrate. Time, from this point, is spatialized, inscribed within an external order of things: in a 'spurious existence', Iqbal comments.[71]

When meditation grasps the inner center within the deep self, the very *élan* of the life of the ego, where what are called states are melted in an indivisible and organic movement, it encounters a unique 'present', the one that is split up by the attention into a series of 'nows' that are substituted for each other successively: it then has the experience of pure duration, of 'time regarded as an organic whole that the Quran describes as 'Taqdir' or the destiny'.[72]

Closely following Bergson's text, Iqbal insists on the free creative movement that is original and that constitutes the universe, things being only what the intelligence carves out, whose more or less stabilized contours it outlines, thus creating the separation that isolates fragments of Reality with a view to the action we carry out on them. But he rejects in Bergson the idea that the analysis of our conscious experience can lead us to the notion of a 'forward rush of the vital impulse' that would be 'wholly arbitrary, undirected, chaotic, and unforeseeable in its behaviour'.[73]

We can understand the rejection of teleology in so far as it represents a de-realization of time, which would only appear as the simple unfolding of a predetermined program. Time is de-realized if it is nothing but the distance that still separates a beginning from a goal which it simply has to seek out, so to speak. There is no longer in this case any *event*, strictly speaking, the future like the past stretching out in a vision that could embrace everything, that of the intelligence that Laplace has spoken of, that knows how to see the end in the beginning.

For Muhammad Iqbal, to not de-realize time is to conceive teleology in a different way starting with the very meaning of what it is to live. The feeling of teleological orientation is identical to the very feeling of life, as 'to live is to shape and change ends and purposes and to be governed by them'.[74] Orientation is not the inexorable realisation of a foreseen end, located at the end of an already-traced line; it should rather be understood as a movement of anticipation and projection, always in the present, which makes time the living and becoming reality of a process that is illuminated by a vision of the future.

And we can understand this non-deterministic teleology, this movement that not only does not deny the open character of the future, but makes this openness its very condition, by mentioning in its regard two notions that are at the heart of another philosophy of action that has already been evoked: that of Gaston Berger. These two notions are that of the *prospective*, which is pursued by this author's phenomenological approach, and that of 'a world that goes toward its youth', according to a Bergerian expression that expresses well what we have called, in Iqbal, 'a cosmology of emergence'.

Gaston Berger has given us a striking image of the prospective: it is the lights required by a car, running faster and faster, after nightfall, on a dark road, which is thus recreated to the extent that it is spread beneath the light that pierces the night.[75] It would thus be incorrect to think that the notion of the prospective is based on foresight. It is, on the contrary, because the world is made of events that we need a notion of prospective attitude that is anticipatory. In Gaston Berger's words: the world is not 'a finite set of problems';[76] on the contrary, each invention only multiplies the possibilities implied in a movement that is accelerating. If to age, then, is to see the possibilities on offer gradually become reduced, as well as one's own ability to take up what comes along, so as to become progressively enclosed within what one is, then the world – and humanity – 'far from aging, is becoming younger and younger'.[77]

A Philosophy of the Individual

These Bergerian notions, which are interconnected, shed a certain amount of light on the Iqbalian thought of the ultimate Reality as 'pure duration in which thought, life and purpose inter-penetrate to form an organic unity', as a 'rationally directed creative life'.[78] And to conceive this life as that of an ego is not a case of anthropomorphism: it is to escape the pantheism of an indifferent entity in order to conceive a genuine Unity that the poet describes as perceiving itself in a more accomplished way, which is to say tests itself, in the mental attitude that is prayer.

Chapter III

A Philosophy of Action

Movement and Action

While the divine 'I am' is 'independent, elemental, absolute',[79] since nothing stands opposed to Him, no 'non-self' confronts Him in its alterity, our 'I am', which makes us be and gauges our level of reality, is held in the relationship, which is constitutive for it, of the self to the non-self. It is for this reason that while its *creative activity*, properly speaking, is nothing other than the very *manifestation* of the Ego as free energy, what properly belongs to the finite ego is *transformative action*. And within this action man will find himself to be free through his participation in the work of God, since this freedom is the very corollary of the cosmology of emergence.

'This necessary relationship between freedom and emergence constitutes the full meaning, for Iqbal, of the story of man's Fall, this fall being itself the translation of the fact that God took a chance on the human ego, which is to say on its freedom. He chose, Iqbal says, to see the emergence of a being endowed with unpredictability, chose 'for finite egos to participate in His life, His power, His freedom'.[80]

In the *Dialogue between God and Man* presented in the poem that bears this title, man becomes aware of the full importance of his transformative action and addresses God with these words:

> You made the night; I made the lamp that lights it up.
> You fashioned clay; I made of it a drinking cup.
> You made the wilderness, the mountain and the steppe;
> I fashioned garden, orchard, avenue and scape.
> I change dread poisons into panaceas, and
> I am the one who fashions mirrors out of sand.[81]

If the infinite Ego is the ultimate 'I am' that combines, outside of any temporal succession, thought, goal and life, the finite ego is, by its very nature, necessarily imperfect insofar as it is a living unity. Its 'I am' is an 'I am' of movement of *aspiration* towards, more unity, towards more consistency, towards a life that would be beyond death's reach, that of a 'conscious, proud and free creature ('Of himself maker, breaker, seer').[82] Self-conscious, proud and free in his transformative action, or rather *through* his transformative action, as it is because he draws glass from stone and turns the poison into an antidote that he says: 'this is me'.

We could then think that the Promethean truth of man is primordially inscribed, in the revolt implied in this posture that expresses the very essence of the ego. And as a matter of fact, in his own revolt the Fallen Angel exalts the greatness he believes he has imparted to the human condition in these terms:

That low-born creature of earth, man,
Of mean intelligence,
Though born in Your lap, will grow old
Under my vigilance.[83]

It is however a matter of understanding that, whatever lesson man may learn from God's Rebel, this will only go in the same direction as his destiny, such as it is inscribed within his primary capacity to receive the gift and responsibility of being a *personality*, within the eminence of his nature that places him at the summit of creation and entrusts him with the role of being vice-gerent: 'For he is the last-born of creation, and before him open up the ages'.[84]

'This is me' thus shows man in the movement of *becoming-individual* and of the self-consciousness of freedom, a movement that sustains all beings and which, in his case alone, gives rise to *personality*. This movement is evolution, whose impetus is the love of the freest and most unique personality: God; and this is why self-consciousness, which constitutes the ego, is also consciousness of the movement that, in humanity alone, reaches a total understanding of itself; and this is why, also, this movement becomes in him an action that posits goals and ends for itself. The finite ego thus is for and through action, according to the force of love that governs the continuous creation of desires and ideals and which has given itself, to this end, the tools of sensibility and reason.

In a letter quoted by his translator, R.A. Nicholson, in the *Introduction* he gives to the English text of the *Secrets of the Self*, Muhammad Iqbal describes this continuous movement of evolution in this way:

Physically as well as spiritually man is a self-contained centre, but he is not yet a complete individual. The greater his distance from God, the less his individuality. He who comes nearest to God is the completest person. Nor that he is finally absorbed in God. On the contrary, he absorbs God into himself. The true person not only absorbs the world of matter; by mastering it he absorbs God Himself into his Ego. Life is a forward assimilative movement. It removes all obstructions in its march by assimilating them. Its essence is the continual creation of desires and ideals, and for the purpose of its preservation and expansion it has invented or developed out of itself certain instruments, e.g., senses, intellect, etc., which help in to assimilate obstructions.[85]

To become more and more of an individual: this assumes that the movement, or what we can call in the language of Schopenhauer, the universal 'will-to-live', becomes directed action. The ultimate end for the finite ego is thus to conquer a personality through its action that has the consistency of a diamond in order to preserve it afterwards, in an immortality which in this way would be snatched from dissolution.

Fatum, Time and Prayer

The Iqbalian philosophy, because it is a thought of emergence and freedom, is opposed to the thesis of a fatalism that is supposed to be inscribed within the very essence of Islam, as well as the metaphysics of a certain Sufism for which life is meditation on death. Thus, only ignorance of the true significance this religion gives to fate has made Islam, for some people, into a fatalism, leading Leibniz for example to refer to *fatum mahometanum* or the '*fatum* of the Turks'.

It is a matter however of thinking in terms of life and movement – 'the thought of death', said Spinoza, 'is not the thought of a living thing' – and of grasping the true sense of fate (*taqdîr*), not in attitudes of passivity and resignation but, for example, in these words spoken by very different men of action: thus Muawiya, the founder of the Omayyad dynasty, proclaimed, 'I am destiny'; 'I am the speaking Quran', declared Ali, the last of the four 'rightly guided caliphs' who succeeded the Prophet at the head of the Islamic community; 'I am a thing, not a person', said Napoleon.

The question of knowing whether human beings are endowed with a free will that would give them control of and responsability for their choices and actions or whether, on the contrary, they are determined to go in one direction or another, is one of the 'philosophical' questions around which the different theological schools in the history of Islamic thought have formed.

Supporters of free will and defenders of determinism have thus opposed each other, each camp being able to cite verses that bolster their position, one presenting itself, ultimately, as the advocate of the Omnipotence of God, the other of His Justice. That determinism and the decrees sealed for all eternity deprive humans of all possibility of being ultimately responsible for their acts, with the result that the reward and punishment of divine Justice become incomprehensible. Or that human beings have, by themselves, the power to choose and to act, with the result that God's Power is hampered, ending where His creatures' powers begin.

Muhammad Iqbal's thoughts on this discussion are expressed, it has been said, in the notion of a risk taken by God on the freedom of the ego. It also takes up, on another level, the position encountered in what can be called 'a Sufism of self-realisation through man's acquisition of divine attributes'.

Thus when the hand that grasps is the hand of God himself, the eye that sees, the eye of God himself, we are led beyond the face-to-face confrontation between determinism and free will by the 'unitive experience' that sees 'the Infinite passing into the loving embrace of the finite'. It is a case of a faith (*imân*) that is not the belief in a set of 'propositions of a certain kind', but an attitude born of a 'living assurance begotten of a rare experience' and which is the state of 'strong personalities'.[86] The 'higher fatalism' implied by this attitude is thus that of people of action, as it is the very feeling of 'life and boundless power which recognizes no obstruction, and can make a man calmly offer his prayers when bullets are showering around him'.[87]

This fatalism of *amor fati*, which belongs to the personality that is truly realised as such, will thus be defined as the feeling that the action involves a living creative force beyond temporal duration. From this point of view, the reversal that can be read in the words of Napoleon cited by Iqbal are particularly instructive: in the awareness of the self as life and power, it is the personality itself that appears as a thing in the hands of its own force.

It is once again Hussein ibn Mansur al- Hallaj, a representative of this Sufism of self-affirmation, who, in the *Book of Eternity*, is given the task of speaking the true meaning of fate and that of the notion of submission which, along with that of peace, is constitutive of the meaning of the term Islam itself. 'Submission' he explains to the poet, 'is not passivity, on the contrary it is a force; not every man, however, he says, 'has the zeal to surrender'.[88] This force must be won, and it is so in the very movement of constitution of a personality that, no longer being dissolved in the back-and-forth between fear and hope, recognizes that the ego is, with itself, in a *peace* that Iqbal also considers to be a 'living assurance' in which its own will bends that of God: 'The true believer', he has Hallaj say, has a sort of understanding with God, and says to him '"We accord with you, so accord with us.' His resolution is the creator of God's determination, and on the day of battle his arrow is God's arrow'.[89]

The arrow here is a reference to the following passage from the Quran (8:17): 'And yet, it was not you who slew the enemy, but it was God who slew them; and it was not thou who cast arrows, when thou didst cast them, but it was God who cast them.' We could also, in the very spirit of Iqbal's 'policy', apply this reading to the following verse: 'God does not change men's condition unless they change their inner selves' (Quran 13:11).

Furthermore, in *Gabriel's Wing*,[90] the poet-philosopher writes: 'Raise your ego to the point where before making your destiny', each time God first asks you, his creature: 'What do you think?'

Not only then has God taken a chance on the freedom of humanity, but He has made the realisation of personality the condition that grants His will to that of the human ego. This is the meaning to give to an active fatalism such as is embodied in the figure of Khâlid ibn al Wâlid. He is known in history by the nickname the 'sword of God' for his military genius both when he was in the armies that, thanks to him, fought victoriously against the first Islamic troops, and when his conversion then put his legendary invincibility at the service of this religion. Hallaj tells the poet that this fatalism of Khâlid's:

turns a world upside down;
for us, constraint tears us up by the roots.
The business of true men is resignation and submission;
this garment does not suit the weaklings.[91]

Fatalism conceived in this way cannot be perverted so that it takes on an aspect of passive resignation to an external will. If such a perversion has happened it is, on the one hand, within a theology that has above all sought to legitimize political states of affairs and, in particular, the dynastic devolution of Omayyad power which was ratified as the expression of the 'will of God'. It is, on the other hand and above all, because the idea of fate has been solely connected to the concept of serial, dividable time, the succession of causes and effects, and not to the one that regards life 'as a whole which in evolving its inner richness creates serial time'.[92]

The fatalism that is perverted in this way is dispossession of self, which is thus based on a conception of time, on a cosmology that presents a universe of closure, where the future, already fixed, is simply held in reserve, so to speak, according to an order of events that is predetermined, inexorable, and which, in the end, fetters even the creative activity of God. This is a case then, in the end, of an astrological cosmology, in which only *foresight* has a meaning, which spreads out a world where time is nothing, deserted as it is by the *élan*, empty of this life translated by the themes that run through Iqbal's poetry: desire, sigh, murmur, drunkenness, thirst, quest, melody, adventure, danger, journey, burning, embraces, love. The poet denounces this imposture: 'Your station, how can the astrologer know it? You are living sediment, you do not depend on the stars'.[93]

When it acts in the world then, positing ends and goals for itself, presenting its surroundings as a system of causes and effects within which it will inscribe its freedom and exercise its initiative, the ego needs to renew its contact with the very source of time, the one that makes it into a factor that participates in the life of the universe. It is through this 'self-possession' that it is able to oppose its dissolution in 'the mechanizing effects of sleep and business': the meaning of prayer is in effect in this 'ego's escape from mechanism to freedom'.[94]

At selected moments then, the ritual will regularly be performed, whose cosmic significance is that of the ego's re-centering itself at the same time as its awareness of being united with a 'larger whole of life'. This awareness is more clearly affirmed in what the tradition considers to be the best form of prayer, that done with others, in which one grasps, or at the very least comes up against, both 'the unity of the all-inclusive Ego who creates and sustains all egos' and 'the essential unity of all mankind', which is felt when, on the same level, shoulder to shoulder, the Brahmin and the untouchable turn towards the same center.[95]

When, in prayer, the ego thus encounters the promise of a larger, fuller, immense life, it understands that the words and gestures that constitute it take on the significance of action. Through prayer as through action then, it participates in the creative activity of God, and each of these fundamental postures of the ego thus illuminates the meaning of the other.

In his novel *Ambiguous Adventure*,[96] Cheikh Hamidou Kane states, 'If a man believes in God, the time he takes from prayer for work is still prayer. It is even a very beautiful prayer.' In this we can see a fundamental idea that goes in the same direction as Iqbalian thought: for this time to be prayer, it must be taken from that given to prayer, not *substituted* for it. This prayer having been deferred, its meaning remains present in the work that defers it. The fact that the transformative action of the person and prayer are two faces of the ego's participation in divine creative activity prevents us from thinking that prayer could be opposed to work (dreamy mysticism) or that work could replace prayer (dissolution in the mechanical and, ultimately, idolatry).

An Ethics of Consumption

In the same way that the mountain without the self is no more than a pile of sand, so, without the cohesive force of the becoming-individual, a human life dissolves in the succession of days that make it up. Thus Ali ibn Abi Tâlib pronounced this 'existentialist' sentence: 'O son of Adam. You are nothing but a collection of days; each day that passes takes away a fraction of your being.'

To make life something other than the sum of its days would be the ultimate significance of human action. In this sense, Iqbal's philosophy of the power of individuation translates into an ethics that rests on the distinction between, on the one hand, what strengthens the ego, which is to say increases its power, and what, on the other hand, diminishes it and thus destroys the ego. This power is once again love. Referring then to an *ergo sum* of love that deserves to be held as a first truth much more than the *ergo sum* of pure thought, the poet thus writes:

> On my existence or my non-existence,
> my thought had its doubts
> It is Love who revealed my secret: I am.[97]

To be is to love; to become an individual is to be consumed, as they say, by love, to know this burning of which Rûmî, in his *Mathnavî*, wrote that it 'is everything, more precious than the world's empire, as it calls God secretly in the night.' It is the poet Georges Bataille who gave 'consumption' *(consumation)* a meaning that can shed light here on the Muhammad Iqbal's suggestion. Edgar Morin explains its meaning, which is 'the fact of burning with a great inner fire', and which is precisely 'the opposite of consuming'.[98] Whereas consuming effectively concerns the accumulation of things around oneself, and, as a result the dispersion or dissipation of the self in things, consumption is the true wealth of the personality which makes it attain itself, forges it in its consistency and expresses it as well, which is to say translates it externally in its signs. In its expression consumption is thus, to use again Edgar Morin's terms, poetry, expenditure, waste, madness...

As it was for Rûmî, who he takes as his master, love appears to Muhammad Iqbal as the royal road, not as a fusional power of self-extinction that annihilates separation, but on the contrary as a force of individuation: 'love individualises the lover as much as the beloved. The effort to realise the most unique individuality individualises the one who seeks and implies the one who is sought, as nothing else will be able to satisfy the nature of the seeker.' Thus comments Javid Iqbal, who cites this passage: 'the despair of separation (from God) is transformed into human joy in distinction (from God) in the Iqbalian conception of love'.[99]

And it is poetry that teaches us to understand this Iqbalian philosophy of love, where difference is joy because it is precisely the sign of inner wealth through love, the very possession of the intimate fire which consumes one. So, even if destitute (in the order of having), the one who loves is always rich from loving (in the order of being), and he spends himself joyfully:

> They say Iqbal, though poor, is generous,
> But has nothing to offer but fire and flames.[100]

The Iqbalian theme of consumption by an inner fire is best expressed, no doubt, in the poetic significance of the glow-worm who sings thus in *The Message from the East*:

> I am not an insect that hurts with its sting.
> One can burn in one's own fire. So do not
> Regard me as a moth that has to fling
> Itself into a flame.
> If the night be
> Dark as deer's eyes, I light my path myself.[101]

The glow-worm (firefly) here is the symbol of consumption, of the inner fire that exhales outward in luminosity, in order to light or rather in order to create the path. It represents the *lucifer* self that realises itself in its own ardor. To this richness of the glow-worm expressed by the luminous profusion that overflows from inside is opposed the ontological poverty of the moth, attracted to the external light and who ends up perishing in the fire. It is called *parvânâ*, which the translators of Gabriel's wing tell us comes from an expression that literally means: the butterfly who jumps on fire and light.[102]

We can then say of Muhammad Iqbal's ethics that it is founded on this poetic ontology of luminosity: beings are more or less luminescent according to the degree of consistency of their ego, thus according to the intensity of their consumption or else – which amounts to the same thing in this philosophy of action where reality is incompletion and change – according to their *power to act*.

As is also the case in Spinoza's philosophy, Iqbalian ethics is above all attention to what, on the one hand, increases one's power to act, and which is thus the
good of the ego (in the sense that it strengthens it) and, on the other, to what is
an evil for it because it corrodes the ego by diminishing its power to act. And the
poets cites, drawing on this way of seeing things, the Quranic verse where God
swears by the soul: 'By the soul and He who hath balanced it, and hath shown it
the ways of wickedness and piety, blessed is he who hath *made it grow* and
undone is he who hath *corrupted* it' (91: 7-10).[103]

Evil is thus never anything but the *self-diminishing* inflicted on oneself, which
can go so far as destruction, when the good is what inscribes the ego within the
significance of the universe of being constant evolution: what makes *the self
grow* to the point of immortality. When Adam and Eve are chased out of Eden,
the prayer they offer up from the depths of their destitution is not to say 'we
have disobeyed your order', which would express remorse at not conforming to
an external transcendent law; but rather to state: 'Lord, we have committed a
wrong against our souls'.

Iqbal suggests then that values are only as they are through the evaluation
that creates them and they must be questioned in function of the intensity of
life they imply. 'Life offers a scope for ego-activity, and death is the first test of
the synthetic activity of the ego. There are no pleasure-giving and pain-giving
acts; there are only ego-sustaining and ego-dissolving acts'.[104]

> And what thus strengthens the ego in the first place, is action, is movement.
> The life of those who are walking on the Path, is to walk and nothing more.
> For waves in movement, there is no stopping, nor rest.
> The burning words of the guide Rûmi illuminated my arid soul: 'The goal of our
> journey, he said, is the Almighty Himself'.[105]

Movement, which is a reality inscribed in cosmic incompletion itself, is also an
ethical imperative that demands that each human act creates a new situation opening
up in turn new opportunities of self-creation in a continuous evolution that is
ultimately the conquest of a life beyond death.

Such is the significance according to Iqbal – for whom resurrection must be
understood as the fine extremity of this movement of intensification of life –
of the Quranic 'demonstration' of a re-emergence of the ego, after the trial that
is death, by analogy with its first creation. He invokes in this regard the following
verses: 'man says, 'What! Once I am dead, shall I again be brought forth alive?'
But does man not bear in mind that We have created him aforetime out of
nothing?' (19: 66-68), 'We have decreed that death shall be among you: but there
is nothing to prevent Us from changing the nature of your existence and bringing
you into being in a manner unknown to you. And you are indeed aware of your
coming into being in the first instance - why, then, do you not bethink yourselves?'
(56: 60-62).

This Iqbalian version of immortality through movement is again inscribed within the evolutionist perspective of the poet Rûmî whose famous lines are recalled:[106]

First man appeared in the class of inorganic things,
Next he passed therefrom into that of plants.
For years he lived as one of the plants,
Remembering nought of his inorganic state so different;
And when he passed from the vegetative to the animal state,
He had no remembrance of his state as a plant,
Except the inclination he felt to the world of plants,
Especially at the time of spring and sweet flowers;
Like the inclination of infants towards their mothers,
Which know not the cause of their inclination to the breast.
Again the great Creator, as you know,
Drew man out of the animal into the human state.
Thus man passed from one order of nature to another,
Till he became wise and knowing and strong as he is now.
Of his first souls he has now no remembrance,
And he will be again changed from his present soul.

A Philosophy of Living

If there is a life after death, it is because there is a life *beyond* death, an enthusiasm for life that the idea of evolution must carry and that one must not thus conceive otherwise than *sub quadam specie aeternitatis*: it is thus not death that destroys the ego in its individuality, it is the ego itself that can lose itself, dissolve its being, which is to say its power to act, in *stagnation*. After that of Spinoza, the Iqbalian philosophy has declared that death does not exist. The only reality of the death of the ego is inactivity, stopping: it is the disintegration that follows the petrification of desire. And strictly speaking, hell does not follow this death since it is itself hell, which is to say, not a *place*, but a *state* which is the horrifying in person, which has nothing to do with tortures inflicted from outside, but with something worse: the feeling itself of failure and the irremediable devastation of meaning when one realises that what one was to be has been emptied of its meaning like water absorbed by sand.

In the same way, heaven is not to be considered as a place of rest where an exhausted faculty of desire would come to lay itself down. This is what has always been understood by the Sufism that refuses to abandon the pursued prey, which is the very Face of God, for the mild shadow of a heaven where one finds everything that one can love, but where loving no longer has any meaning. 'You have no desire for wine, nor gaze for my beauty. It is strange that you know nothing of love', says the *houri* to the poet, who retorts that 'rest is ... death', as: 'The heart of a lover could not live in eternal paradise: where there is neither sorrowful song, nor grief, nor confidant'.[107]

We must thus see something else behind the sensory images presented by the notions of eternal torment or endless bliss in Edenic rest. It is in the nature of the living sediment that is man to bring himself back again from the deepest failure; the feeling of having committed a wrong against oneself can prove to be 'a corrective experience which may make a hardened ego once more sensitive to the living breeze of Divine Grace'.[108] In the same way, 'Heaven is the joy of triumph over the forces of disintegration', and this joy is itself the power to act for the ego who always 'marches onward' and creates itself continuously in actions that, in turn, then open 'further opportunities of creative unfolding'.[109]

We cannot fail to see the presence of Kant in this Iqbalian thought of immortality. No doubt the poet has in mind the passage from the third section of the *Critique of Practical Reason* concerning 'the dialectic of pure practical reason' where Kant speaks of the 'paradise of Muhammad.' In the Kantian text, this represents a 'monstrous' perversion – since it is constituted of 'dreams' riddled through and through with a material appetite for pleasure – of the practical ideal of the Sovereign Good. Sufism, it has been said, has always recalled that we must know how to understand the description of the state of paradise so that we do not make it, in a contradictory way, into an obstacle to love. Islamic modernist philosophy has also returned to the question to indicate the spiritual interpretation that should be given of it.[110]

Iqbal goes further than this simple spiritualization by bringing the question to bear on immortality itself. He thus discusses different conceptions of personal immortality and different arguments in its favor. And, first of all, the Kantian ethical argument that posits as a practical postulate, on the one hand the reality of this immortality of the soul that alone permits an indefinite progress toward the ideal of holiness; and on the other the reality of Being that alone is in a position to grant, in order to thus accomplish the sovereign good, happiness to morality, which is to say God. Iqbal wonders then why the indefiniteness of the time required for the achievement of the supreme good would be the infinity of immortality, or again what could be the content of this divine synthesis of virtue and happiness, that are heterogeneous to each other, in this philosophical appropriation – within the limits of reason alone – of religious representations.[111]

Following this brief discussion of the Kantian conception of immortality as postulate of practical reason in the *Lecture* devoted to the human ego, comes that of the Nietzchean eternal return. It is a case of poetic inspiration but also of a despairing idea, according to Iqbal, of immortality, which doesn't succeed in shedding any light on the perspective of the arrival of the overman: this ideal combination, like all the others, has already taken place an infinity of times, it does not bring about any radical novelty, and the eternal return hardly has the vital value it is supposed to carry: the overman who only returns to the same does not accomplish the work that justifies him being the promise borne by man: the achievement of the world, to use a concept of Teilhard de Chardin's.

These lines in fact by the author of *Milieu divin*, are entirely appropriate to Muhammad Iqbal's thought:[112] 'we must all, in the course of our lives, not only show ourselves obedient and docile. But by our fidelity we must build – starting with the most natural territory of our own selves – a work, an *opus*, into which something enters of all the elements of the earth. We make our own soul throughout our earthly lives; and at the same time we collaborate in another work, another *opus*, which infinitely transcends, while at the same time it narrowly determines, the perspectives of our individual achievement: the completion of the world'.

To collaborate in the achievement of the world, such is the mission of the overman, which must be understood not as aiming for the closure of this world, but rather its opening; which must thus be understood as the invention of new possibilities of life, to precisely speak like Nietzsche.[113]

The figure of Nietzsche is very present in Iqbal's work. However, it represents more of a poetic theme than a philosophy that would be referred to and eventually discussed for itself. Thus, for example, in the *Book of Eternity*, the German philosopher has his home 'beyond the spheres' and is introduced to the poet by his guide Rûmî as 'a Hallaj who was a stranger in his own city; he saved his life from the mullahs, and the physicians slew him', he whose 'eyes desired no other vision but man' and who 'fearlessly ... shouted: 'Where is Man?''[114]

The overman is not the representative of a higher humanity. He is humanity, in achieved form. What Muhammad Iqbal says, sometimes in the language of the author of *Zarathustra*, regarding this collaborator in God's *opus* who tirelessly works to be equal to his infinite responsibility and task of achieving the world has, in fact, less to do with Nietzsche's overman than with 'the perfect man' – *perfectus* – of the Sufi tradition: the *insân al-kâmil*, the idea of which is associated with Abd al-Karîm al Jîlî, the author whose major work bears this title.

It must moreover be specified that the idea of the overman such as it appears in Iqbal is above all Quranic and that its significance is simply that of being the goal of this tendency in the human being, that is its life itself and its greatness, toward the creation within him of divine attributes. Thus the Earth he inhabits, whose achievement is his task, will respond thanks to him to the contempt shown to it by Heaven from the first day of creation, and the angels' prophecy will thus be realised:

> The lustre of a handful of earth one day shall outshine the creatures of light;
> earth through the star of his destiny one day shall be transformed into heaven.
> His imagination, which is nourished by the torrent of vicissitudes,
> one day shall soar out of the whirlpool of the azure sky.
> Consider one moment the meaning of Man; what thing do you ask of us?
> Now he is pricking into nature, one day he will be modulated perfectly,
> so perfectly modulated will this precious subject be that even the heart of
> God will bleed one day at the impact of it![115]

This idea of the overman inscribed within man as his destiny gives man all of his dignity and installs the respect of man at the outset of any morality. Because he represents the universal Man in his own person, the Prophet is the one who makes humanity an *oeuvre*: his retreat, Iqbal, has given rise to a people.[116] And when the poet proclaims: 'Say I, you can deny God, but you cannot deny the dignity of the Prophet!', we may understand by this that if we think we can doubt God in His transcendence, we cannot fail to encounter Him in the greatness of Man; and this is also perhaps why it is said of this Prophet – and the Quran insists on his simple humanity – that God Himself and His angels pray upon him.

The ethical undertaking to bring Man about means to strengthen the ego against dissolving influences. In his presentation of the Iqbalian conception of the ego, Javid Iqbal lists the factors that increase its power to act and which, for this reason, represent ethical values: it is a matter, he says, of love, freedom, courage and disinterestedness, and he insists on this point, which is effectively essential, that it is a case here of values of individuality. We find in Anwarul Haq's reflection on the human ego in Muhammad Iqbal's philosophy a more detailed enumeration of the forces that enhance the consistency of the personality. They are, according to the list he presents: (i) love, (ii) *faqr*, (iii) courage, (iv) tolerance, (v) *kasb-hilal*, (vi) original and creative activity. Conversely, he writes, the dissolving influences that diminish the power to act are: (i) fear, (ii) beggary or *sawal*, (iii) servitude and (iv) the exaltation of belonging or *nasab parasti*.[117]

In the end, this opposition between strengthening and dissolving factors comes to a great extent down to that between *faqr*, which is freedom and *sawal*, which is servitude, between poverty and neediness. This is a case of an opposition which itself is clarified by everything that the Sufi tradition places under this notion of *faqr*. The poverty in question here is that of *disinterestedness*, which is to say that which precisely *asks for* nothing.

To demand diminishes the self. This could be the fundamental statement of the Iqbalian ethic. The demand has the sense of a mode of being which belongs to a diminished, stunted soul; it is the dispossession of self, the very expression of what Muhammad Iqbal calls, following Nietzsche, a 'slave' morality. To demand is to hold out one's hand, of course, but it is above all and more fundamentally to adopt a posture in the world of which this attitude is the sign: that which consists in expecting time to provide the means and reasons to live. The one who demands thus places themselves before time and life as before a distribution of lots, in a position that gives rise to everything that the self can *poison itself* with: fatalism, fear, jealousy, envy; in a word, once again Nietzschean: *ressentiment*.

To imitate is thus also to demand; to shape life within the mould of indefinitely repeated habits, received ideas that are petrified into certainties, the *taqlid* (servile imitation of the past) that is denounced by philosophy as well as Sufism, this has the effect of dissolving personality. And this is apparent in the fact that imitation is precisely the opposite of the original and creative activity that features in the list of values that strengthen the ego. This activity is nothing other, in effect, than the courage to live, the enthusiasm for life and freedom: as such it is opposed to the laziness, the fear of living, which is to say of inventing, of the one who shuts themselves up in the time of repetition, imitation, servitude.

'To live is not to live if one lives without danger', writes Iqbal in *The Mysteries of Selflessness*. Muhammad Iqbal's taking up of this idea of *living dangerously*, far from having the meaning of a daredevil formula, is thus the very expression of a philosophy of creation of an 'artist philosophy'. And we can also understand why, in the list of the dissolving influences on the ego, fear comes in first place. It is through fear in fact that the idea of death enters into a world which is life through and through. It is, Iqbal says, 'a spy come from the world of Death' and he makes it the source of all of the dissolving influences which, ultimately, only represent different modalities of fear:

> Whatever evil lurks within thy heart
> Thou cast be certain that its origin Is fear.[118]

It is for this reason that the figure of the predatory animal is often encountered in Iqbal's poetry – the lion, the eagle, the falcon, the sparrowhawk – representing the refusal of all imprisonment and thus presenting the very figure of freedom and disinterestedness.[119]

A Philosophy of Tolerance

We must also understand 'the exaltation of belonging' as an imprisonment of the self, a true servitude that diminishes the power to act. For it is still servitude to substitute, for the movement of *self-invention*, the process of 'becoming-someone', which is human identity itself, the *belonging* to a tribe, to a caste, from which one demands guidelines for pre-established ways of living and thinking.

In his own country, with the hierarchical system of castes that characterizes it, the message of the 'Brahmin' Iqbal is undoubtedly important on the social and political level. It is a matter of renouncing the pride of birth, he clearly indicates, as:

> There are neither Afghans, nor Turks, nor sons of Tartar,
> We are all the fruits of a single garden,
> a single trunk,
> We are the flowering of a same spring.[120]

This social message itself follows from the Iqbalian philosophy and ethics of the 'becoming-someone' in which the confusion between the movement of identity and the imprisonment within belonging is, quite simply, the supreme sin of idolatry: – 'Break all the idols of tribe and caste Break the ancient customs which enchain men!'[121] – which risks shielding from your own eyes the mission you must respond to, one aspect of which is the achievement of the world and the other the invention of the self.

Also as a result we may consider as idolatry everything that goes against a principle of tolerance that can be said to be *active*, which is to say is based on the idea that identity is not being closed in on oneself but the ability to welcome difference. And this cannot be fully understood in effect except within a philosophy of impermanence, in a philosophy that is thus able to be *restless* with God and truth.

It is thus not surprising to read from the pen of this disciple of Rûmî's that:

> The one who loves finds no difference between the Ka'aba
> and the Temple of idols:
> The first is the apparition of the Friend, the second is his sanctuary.[122]

But perhaps the best illustration of what a tolerance that can welcome difference can mean is in a way, that we can call Iqbalian in spirit, of understanding the tradition according to which there are seventy-two Islamic sects, only one of which is destined to be saved. Taking up this prophetic saying in his poetry, Iqbal writes:

> The true doctrine is lost in the quarrels
> of the seventy-two sects:
> Impossible to understand it if your perception
> is not impartial![123]

Ghazâlî, in his treaty entitled *Deliverance from Error*, begins the presentation of his search for the truth, beyond the schools, doctrines and controversies which, at the time he was writing, divided minds and hearts, by recalling this tradition of the seventy-two sects (there is a variation that refers to seventy-three sects and this is the one used in Ghazâlî's text); and to emphasize the dramatic nature of his path, at the end of which salvation is at stake, he immediately adds afterwards: 'this saying is about to be realised'.

There is a primary *sectarian*, way of understanding this saying: the one that would look for the group, among the seventy-two or seventy-three, that would hold the correct point of view. If this approach, in the best of cases, could lead to the sect that is considered to be the right one to *tolerate* the others, this would be in a condescending way, accepting to suffer them. A second way, which corresponds to what has been called an active tolerance, consists of understanding this tradition as a parable designed to test 'the impartial perception' of the truth by the testing of the self. It will then precisely be a matter, by means of the alterity and the questioning it bears, of knowing how to go beyond oneself to question belonging and test certainties.

Following this second approach, we can then understand that difference is an invitation to a dialogue with oneself as well, with oneself above all, and that it is the shortest route in the knowledge and strengthening of the self. This approach would not be relativistic or sceptical, considering for example that the truth is nothing but error seen from another angle: on the contrary, it will be assured in itself because of its attentiveness to the different faces under which the same truth is able to draw its adherents. In a word, it will be understood that the sect that will be saved is the one that would have attained, through the deepening of the self as well as the *restlessness* of difference, the *impartial percep-tion* of the truth and which would be virtually *inscribed within each* of the seventy-two or seventy-three. And we will also understand, with the poet, that this *non-sectarian approach* must be followed not only in the world of Islamic sects but in the world in general.

A Politics of Autonomy

To speak of Muhammad Iqbal's philosophy of action is also to ask what light it can shed on his effective political action in the years of torment that led to the separate independences of India and Pakistan.

Let us dwell for a moment on the Iqbal who appears as a character in Hélène Cixous' play, *L'Indiade ou l'Inde de leurs rêves*.[124] There he is the one who stubbornly insinuates his idea of an Islamic state separate from Hindu India in the spirit of Muhammad Ali Jinnah (1876–1948), who will later become the *Quaid i-Azam* or Grand Leader, the founder of Pakistan. And since he ends up convincing Jinnah of the necessity of the partition despite the prayers and infinite love of the Mahatma Gandhi himself, his character in the play is quite that of a 'evil influence'.

As a matter of fact, in his Introduction to the *Letters*[125] that Iqbal wrote to him during the years of struggle for independence, Muhammad Ali Jinnah makes the ideas of the poet-philosopher the very foundation of the will to create an Islamic state separate from the mostly Hindu India, and which was expressed in detail in the Lahore Resolution of the Pan-Indian Muslim League of 1940, also known as the 'Pakistan Resolution'. And, in a message on the occasion of the Iqbal Day celebrated in Lahore in 1944, he presented the ideas and political actions of Muhammad Iqbal in the following terms:

> Iqbal was not only a preacher and a philosopher ... He combined within himself the idealism of the poet and the realism of the man who takes a practical approach to things ... Even though he was a great poet and a great philosopher, he was no less a practical politician ... he was one of those very small number of men who were the first to consider the possibility of carving out, in the north-west and north-east of India, an Islamic state, these regions which are historically Islamic lands.[126]

This appreciation can be usefully contrasted with that of those who criticized the poet's action in the early thirties, precisely considering that this betrayed his poetry and his philosophy. A journalist from the *Bombay Chronicle* thus set himself up, in an interview with him on the eve of his departure to attend then round table of 1931, as the spokesperson for these critics. What would he say, he thus asked, to those who found his former attitude (judged to be separatist and finally compliant to the interests of the British colonial powers) difficult to understand and in contradiction with the teachings of his poetry? Who considered that Iqbal the politician had taken over Iqbal the poet, whom he hardly resembled anymore?[127] It can also be recalled in this regard that he himself declared – in 1910 it is true, which is to say before the end, in 1926, of what has been called the (certainly turbulent) 'honeymoon'[128] between Hindus and Muslims: 'nations are born in the hearts of poets; they prosper then die in the hands of politicians.'[129]

It is finally useful, when we thus consider the different evaluations made of Iqbal's political action, to recall what the judgement of Jawaharlal Nehru was as we can read in his work *The Discovery of India*.[130] 'If Iqbal', he writes in this book, 'was one of the first advocates of Pakistan, it appears he had different ideas at the end of his life'. He recounts that, having made the journey to Iqbal's sickbed – it is Iqbal who summoned him – he had a talk with him that reminded them of how much they had in common and at the end of which the poet declared to him: 'what do you and Jinnah have in common? He is a politician, you are a patriot'.[131]

But if we attend to the facts themselves, the chapter that Lini S. May entitled 'the march towards independence' in the work that she devoted to Iqbal shows perfectly well his insistence – he begs pardon from Jinnah at one point for writing so often to a man that he knows, he says, to be so busy – but that he is the only one 'India's Islamic community has the right to ask for safe guidance in the storm that will strike the north-west region and perhaps the whole of India'.[132] Muhammad Ali Jinnah, his biographers indicate, began his political career showing the most ferocious will to forge unity between Hindu and Muslim Indians. At the end of the first ten years of this career, from 1906 to 1916, this attitude had earned him the nickname 'the ambassador of Hindu-Muslim unity' and Sarojini Naidu, who in 1918 published a text precisely called *Mohomed Ali Jinnah: An Ambassador of Unity*, said of him that he was 'not only an ambassador but the living symbol Hindu-Muslim unity'.[133] Still in 1937, in a speech he made during March in Delhi, if he speaks of the separate organization of Hindus and Muslims, it is in order, he says, 'to better favor their mutual understanding in the "national fight"'.[134] It is to this man that Iqbal will insist, to convince him of the idea that he will express forcefully in 1940 as president of the Muslim League: 'No force on earth can prevent Pakistan.'

How are we to understand in the end the trajectory that led Iqbal to the imperative of autonomy? Shall we say that alongside the essential aim of the poet and the philosopher, and thus externally in relation to this aim, circumstances ended up imposing on him the realism and practical outlook of the politician, thus leading him to conceive and even to sketch out the Pakistan that was realised after his death? Shall we thus evoke the *force of circumstance*? Shall we not rather look for an internal, necessary relationship between the Iqbalian philosophy of the 'reconstruction of religious thought in Islam' around the notion of self-affirmation, whether as individual or collective ego, and the political demand for autonomy? He himself provided an answer to these questions, forming the subject of the important historical text that is the speech he made as session President to the Muslim League at its 29 December 1930 meeting in Allahabad. And this speech intimately blends the force of circumstance and the necessity of the idea.

In his presentation,[135] Iqbal begins by stressing the fact that he himself is in no way a political man but a scholar who, as a result of having spent most of his life studying Islam in its laws, institutions, history and culture, considers himself to be in a position and under an obligation to shed light on the decisions that are for the members of the League to make. The question he then raises is that of the very nature of religion: 'can we consider', he asks, 'that it is simply a private matter, the lived experience of the individual alone who has decided to split himself between his spiritual and his temporal life?' In Islamic thought, he declares in response to this question, the dualism between spirit and matter that grounds such a separation hardly corresponds to the reality of a religious ideal that created a social order to which it remains organically attached.

Then comes, in his ideas, the question of the nation, in relation to which he recalls the concept used by Renan to define it: that of the 'moral consciousness' that is constitutive of it, beyond any particular cultural attachments. Ultimately this question is that of knowing what nation to conceive. Is there thus a genuine 'moral consciousness' behind the idea, that we could call 'pan-Indian', of the nation? Conversely, can pan-Islamic nationalism truly have a content in the present circumstances? In a certain way, the future Pakistan will be built against these two nationalisms.

On the one side, against the Indian nationalist movement, for which the essential thing was the struggle against imperialism, which assumed the divisions of religious communitarianism to be genuinely overcome in the spirit of the Lucknow Pact of 1916, by which Hindus and Muslims were to demand India's autonomy together. On the other side, against a pan-Islamic nationalism manifesting itself, for example, in the 'Khilafat Conference' party founded by Muhammad Ali (1879-1930) in 1919, whose action would be directed by the principle of 'non-cooperation' undertaken by Gandhi. The explicit objective of the Khilafat Conference was to obtain the full restoration of the Ottoman Empire by pressuring colonial powers: how could one fight for the independence of a given territory, of only a portion of the Community of Believers (*Ummah*), forgetting Muslim lands in general – especially those where the holy places of Islam are located – as well as the caliphal power of the Ottomans that could be considered to be the very symbol and rallying point of this community? Historians often cite this image used by Muhammad Ali to convey his emotion and his confusion: his belonging to two non-concentric circles, one of which is India, the other the Islamic world.

What were the circumstances? In Turkey, it was the secularist movement of Mustapha Kemal who in 1924 abolished the caliphate, returning in a certain way the pan-Islamic movements to the inevitable reality of nations. In India itself, despite the sadness and hunger strikes of Mahatma Gandhi, inter-communal tensions seemed more and more to confirm the conclusion of the report prepared in 1934 on Indian constitutional reforms: considering in effect that, behind the anti-colonial struggle for independence, one was also confronted with the antagonism not only between two religions, but between two veritable 'civilizations'.

In his work entitled *The Illusion of Cultural Identity*,[136] Jean-François Bayart describes perfectly the mechanism by which primordial identities are manufactured, which very often harden into veritable 'civilizations' in conflict. And in order to account for this mechanism, he very rightly uses a chemical concept, speaking of the '*precipitation* of communalism'.[137] Referring more specifically to the clash between Hindu and Muslim nationalisms which finally led to what Hindus considered to be the 'sacrilege of Mother India's vivisection',[138] Jean-François Bayart writes:

> the fabrication of Vedic authenticity, by 'assimilating the Other's values' has provided a vehicle for a radical mutation of Hindu cultural identity and its politicization in a nationalist manner. For its part, Islam in the Indian subcontinent has not proven to be either more united or more stable than Hinduism, no matter how Hindu nationalists have perceived it. In India, communalism is fed not by the internal coherence of the two religious communities, but precisely by their relationship, which has been an antagonistic one in certain situations and historical periods. However, it should be stressed that this antagonism is not immanent to their respective dogmas, or to their encounter in an enlarged polity constructed by the colonizing power.[139]

The 'force of circumstance' is thus legible no doubt in this permanent clash of nationalisms which were hardened in their mirroring of each other, so to speak. This is what led Iqbal to write in a letter, and this was already in 1909, that 'the vision of a common Indian nation is a *beautiful ideal with poetic appeal*, but which, when one considers the present conditions as well as the unconscious tendencies at the heart of both communities, appears impossible to realise.'[140]

To return to Iqbal's speech to the Muslim League, we can note that he persistently returns to this feeling of a sort of inevitability of communalism, formed, he says, from the suspicion and distrust of each of the communities, Hindu and Muslim, toward the other. This mirroring relationship, he says, leads to the adoption of the narrow-minded attitude of the caste or the tribe.[141] But he raises this to immediately add that there is a higher aspect of communalism, he says, that makes him 'love' the group thus formed: this aspect corresponds to the necessary cultural autonomy that alone can allow, he declares, a given community to 'work out the possibilities that may be latent in it.'[142] It is thus because Islamic religious thought must engage in its own reconstruction, which is above all that of its law, that the *federalist* demand he advocated at that point in time does not constitute in his eyes the sign of an identitarian rigidity but, on the contrary, the condition of the self-creating movement that precisely needs *autonomy*. And in the same presentation, Iqbal indicates all of the importance that this movement of reconstruction that would take place in the most populous territory in the Muslim world would have for the whole of Islam. Thus, fully aware of the emergence of a force of renewal in the Indian sub-continent, Iqbal declares that this would be 'for Islam, an opportunity to rid itself of the stamp that Arabian Imperialism was forced to give it, to mobilise its law, its education, its culture, and to bring them into closer contact with its own original spirit and with the spirit of modern times.'[143]

Overall, *autonomy* is conceived above all for and by *ijtihâd*, which is to say the effort of innovation: autonomy is thus both the condition and the meaning of the movement of continuous self-creation. And we can say that this was the principal lesson, for the poet, of the two revolutions that had a great resonance in his work, that of October and that of Mustafa Kemal Atatürk.

From the October revolution and the socialist ideal it sought to express what Iqbal essentially retained as the goal of *self-repossession*. Thus, 'The Song of the Worker', a poem contained in *Message from the East*, expresses a rather poetic vision of the imperative carried in the conditions of the proletariat: it is a matter, against the alienation brought by capitalism, of no longer 'living unconscious of oneself' like – according to a frequent image in his poetry – the 'butterfly' who lives 'fluttering around the flame'.[144] And it is the same poetic theme that we find when it is a matter for the philosopher of evoking the condition of the Muslim who has 'become a stranger to himself', according to the three possible meanings of this state of alienation: that connected to the colonial situation to which Muslim countries are subject, that – an effect of the first – consisting in the pure and simple imitation of the West and that, finally, expresses the fact of being cut off from the very principle of one's movement. The figure of this last meaning of self-forgetting, to which all are ultimately related, is *petrification, immobilism*.

This is why Muhammad Iqbal, citing large extracts from the texts of the Turkish nationalist poet Zia, 'whose songs', he writes, 'inspired by the philosophy of Auguste Comte, have done a great deal in shaping the present thought of Turkey', shares this poet's observation that 'among the Muslim nations of today, Turkey alone has shaken off its dogmatic slumber and attained to self-consciousness'.[145]

To attain to self-consciousness is the primary philosophical imperative and also constitutes the aim of politics: this must aim at autonomy understood as the implementation of power, or rather of the *duty of ijtihâd*, in order to give society back its ability to pursue its own principle within the indefinitely open process of its continuous auto-creation. This is why, at the end of his life, at the same time that he emphatically demands that Jinnah become the spokesperson of the autonomist imperative, he undertakes preparations for new work that was to be a sequel to his *Lectures* and that he would not have time to write: a work he wanted to be 'an introduction to the study of Islam with particular emphasis on its jurisprudence'[146] and which was described by his secretary at the time who wrote down the outlined plan for the book as a work 'destined to be definitive, a reference work in the area of Islamic institutions and jurisprudence'.[147]

In the principle of this politics of autonomy we find the cosmology of emergence on which Iqbalian thought is founded. And it is this cosmology which demands that each generation is able, of course, to draw on what preceding generations have thought and done, but in understanding the necessity it finds itself in of inventing, in *fidelity* but also in *movement*, the solutions to bring to its own problems. In practice, Iqbal indicates, this means the establishment of legislative assemblies that organise the *ijtihâd*, the 'republican form of government' having become a necessity in virtue of the new forces that are liberated, he says, in the Islamic world. In this way, finally, the world of Islam in its diversity and in its unity will henceforth present itself no longer as a group governed by a caliph, but as a 'living family of republics'.[148]

Chapter IV

Fidelity and Movement

On Science

In his monumental *History of Islamic Philosophy*, Majid Fakhry has Muhammad Iqbal occupy a prominent position among the representatives of 'modernism', at the heart of a line in which one encounters the names of the Persian reformer Djamal al-Dîn al Afghânî (1839–1897), who can be considered as the spiritual father of this current of thought, the Egyptian Muhammad Abduh (1849–1905), a disciple of the first, or, in India, Sayyid Ahmad Khan (1817–1898) and Sayyid Amir Ali (1849–1928).

One of the essential characteristics of the 'modernist' attitude is, in his opinion, the insistence of thinkers in this current on the conjunction between religion and science, and on the role of the spirit of research and analysis in the development of civilization.[149] Thus, for example, in his *Presentation of the Muslim Religion*,[150] Muhammad Abduh writes that it is 'in the nature of man to be guided by science' – the science of the universe, he specifies – 'and the knowledge of things of the past'.[151] He recalls the suggestion of a 'contemporary Western philosopher' according to whom civilization developed in Europe when it was based on 'the emancipation of the will and independence in judgement', two principles that allowed many minds to 'become acquainted' and 'acknowledge in each other the right to exercise their will and seek the truth under the guidance of their reason'; and he adds that 'the philosopher in question specified that it was a ray of light from Islamic culture and Muslim science that enlightened them in the 16th century'.[152]

It must be said that this recollection of a period when the spirit of inquiry and free thought were honored in the Islamic world, and which then contributed to their development in Europe, is common in those thinkers called 'modernist' and in particular represents an important aspect of Muhammad Iqbal's position.

But in other respects Majid Fakhry also expresses a certain irritation with the place and role that science holds, according to him, in Islamic modernist thought. And it is with particular regard to Muhammad Iqbal, he says, given his universality of spirit as well as the learning and eclecticism shown in the references he introduces into his arguments – Fakhry considers them to be sometimes 'exasperating' – that he denounces what he considers to be the mistake of the modernists in general: 'By joining the Islamic or Quranic conception of man and the world to the current stage of scientific development, as Iqbal did particularly, the modernists make a ... very dangerous mistake, since they subordinate the religious truth of Islam to the doubtful truth of a scientific phase. And if the history of scientific progress teaches us anything, it is the ephemeral nature of such scientific phases, whether they are associated with the venerable names of Aristotle or Ptolemy or with the modern pioneers such as Newton, Eddington or Einstein'.[153]

In a word, there is thus a scientistic and obscurantistic way of referring to scientific discourse; and, at the end of this criticism, is perhaps indeed found the idea that, on this level, modernism runs a high risk of being nothing but a scientism, a simple varnish composed of allusions, gratuitous in the end, to a scientific juncture that is essentially changeable. There would in this case be the danger of misunderstanding the non-fluctuating truth of the religious domain.

It is an important criticism: we only have to remember the Galileo affair to be convinced of it. The question also appears to be very current when it is connected to the quite definitely scientistic sort of exegeses that are encountered with many contemporary authors, which consist in reading, in passages of the Quran that are then considered to be 'scientific', the prefiguration and something like the *key* to today's discoveries or theories.

That, effectively, unlike Iqbal's discourse on science, is scientism, which wants in some a way for the Book to also be a – coded – scientific treatise, the code never being deciphered except retrospectively of course, once the theory has been produced. This type of approach is built on free interpretations at the end of which one is flabbergasted to find in such or such a verse the very thing one has put there oneself, in the will to see at any price scientific anticipations in the Quranic text.[154]

We certainly find, here and there, formulations that seem to support the idea that the reference to science fills, in Muhammad Iqbal's philosophical position, such a role of confirmation, which would thus make him vulnerable to Majid Fakhry's criticism. It is thus necessary to examine things in detail, and judge the use that is made of science in specific cases: after evoking the identification of God with light, as it is encountered in the three monotheisms, Muhammad Iqbal reminds us that 'The teaching of modern physics is that the velocity of light cannot be exceeded and is the same for all observers whatever their own system of movement. Thus, in the world of change, light is the nearest approach to the Absolute'.[155]

On analysis, we can clearly see that here there is neither the idea of religious discourse anticipating that of science nor of the confirmation of the former by the latter. It is simply a case of knowing that today our situation is one of living in a world where the theory of relativity tells us something about light that can impart new depth to our way of understanding, which is to say of interpreting, the words that identify God with 'the light of the Heavens and of the earth'. In other words, what is expressed in the scientific reference is neither a simple inessential varnish, nor an 'intellectual imposture' that would seek to import scientific discourse by claiming to be unaware of the boundary that separates it from philosophy. It is the *reconstruction*, in the present of a state of culture that is also connected to a given arrangement of scientific knowledge, of our reading and interpreting tools and protocols of words that, thereby, remain living, which is to say open.

This concept of 'reconstruction', featured in the title of his major work, is, in effect, important in Iqbal's thought. It also carries the sense of a 'revitalization' whose necessity, to take an older example, was apparent to Ghazâlî at the end of the task he undertook to place in doubt the authority of the tradition insofar as it led only to imitation and conformism. We find this concept in Muhammad Iqbal's writing when he speaks of a 'work of reconstruction' of a theory that characterized a theological school within Islam, known under the name of 'Ash'arite atomism', 'in the light of modern physics'.[156]

That the atomism of the Ash'arite *kalâm*[157] does not prefigure such or such an aspect of modern physics goes without saying, as it also goes without saying that he does not find any miraculous confirmation in it. In a word, it must be understood that its justification pertains entirely to the metaphysical questions he has been seeking to formulate a response to, and nothing to do with this physics. Given, in the light of this physics, it can be reinterpreted, take on a new life, be reconstructed as a theory that speaks to us today. And there we have the whole content of the Iqbalian notion of 'reconstruction', which gives its meaning to the whole approach of the poet-philosopher. Iqbal defines this approach by writing that 'equipped with penetrative thought and *fresh experience* the world of Islam should courageously proceed to the work of reconstruction before them'.[158]

The first and principal merit of the Ash'arite theory in Iqbal's eyes is that of having constituted within the history of Islamic thought, the moment of systematic refusal of a complete and fixed world. In effect, new atoms are produced every instant which augment a universe that is nothing other than continuously active creative energy become visible. In this universe, a thing, as a result, is 'in its essential nature an aggregation of atomic acts'.[159] We can thereby see what 'illumination' this Ash'arite atomism might receive when it is considered in a light educated by what modern physics says about leaps, discontinuity, etc.: the cosmology of emergence whose importance in Iqbal's philosophy has been stated is not genuinely conceivable until a non-Newtonian physics is possible, and this in turn allows us to read, reconstructing its meaning retrospectively, the atomistic doctrine developed by Ash'arite theology.

But the essential point regarding the significance of the role of scientific discourse in Iqbal's philosophical position lies elsewhere: what is truly important is less the reference to this discourse than, in the words of the physicist Abdus Salâm, the fact of 'introducing accepted scientific knowledges and concepts into the life of the community'[160]; thus moving to the reappropriation of the scientific spirit by Muslim societies, which represents one of the conditions of possibility of *ijtihâd*.

This imperative, which is effectively a constant with the 'modernists', can be considered as an extension of the debate around the relationship between the scientific spirit and Islam, such as took place, for example, following a lecture by Ernest Renan, that saw contributions from, among others, Al Afghânî and the writer Charles Mismer, in France, in 1883.

In his 'Réponse Al Afghânî' that appeared in the *Journal des Débats* of 19 May 1883, Ernest Renan indicated that it was precisely his conversation with Afghânî, to whom he had just been introduced, that convinced him to choose to speak, in a famous lecture delivered at the Sorbonne, on 'L'Islamisme et la Science'. This lecture, published afterwards, 30 March 1883, in the *Journal des Débats*, gave rise to many responses, including that from Al Afghânî.

Renan's thesis on Islam is well known: on the metaphysical and theological level, he positively appraises the demanding and minimalist character of Islamic monotheism, and, in particular, the fact that the Muslim religion is not based on miracles and the supernatural, and that it is consequently careful not to confuse faith with the sense of the marvellous; but it seems to him that, when it comes to the scientific spirit, the rational imperative stops, and with it curiosity: it is necessary in effect, he believes, to know how to avoid the science of nature being in competition with God.

Against this thesis was the reaction of Charles Mismer, who wrote regarding Renan's lecture that it was 'a work of pure eloquence, suspended on needle-points';[161] and thus opposing this presentation of an Islam that would be inherently resistant to the spirit of scientific inquiry, he referred to a necessary 'regeneration of Islam' in these terms: 'Islam is like a clock whose mechanism is intact, even though it is obstructed by rust and dust. All that is needed is to shake off the dust, remove the rust and set the pendulum in motion to rally the seventh part of humanity round the time of science and civilization'.[162]

In these two ways of seeing was the opposition between an essentialist approach – that of Renan – and a genuinely historical approach, which is Charles Mismer's. If Renan's thesis ultimately amounted to turning the real, given situation of Muslim societies at the time he was writing into the very essence of their religion, Mismer's response and the metaphor of the clock that expresses it is based rather on the historical fact of a prior development of the sciences in the Islamic world.

Many were greatly astonished, and some offended, during this debate, by the particularly moderate and conciliatory position adopted by Djamal al-Dîn al Afghânî regarding Renan's statements.[163] We can understand as reasons for this, firstly, that he took the lecturer's thesis as a description of the Muslim societies of the end of the nineteenth century, regarding which he himself, in many places in his work, had written, from this perspective, the same thing as the French philosopher, often citing the verse from the Quran according to which 'God does not change men's condition unless they change their inner selves' (13:11).

We may remark here that this attitude of Al Afghânî's regarding Renan, reproduced Iqbal's attitude to Spengler's 'culturalism', which consists in conceiving civilizations as separate organisms, as so many juxtaposed and incommunicable islands, each one enclosed within its own context and ultimately depending only on its own specific principle of evolution. Spengler thus, says Iqbal, mistakes the 'magian crust' overlaying Muslim societies today for the very expression of a *magian spirit* that would be the *essential* feature of Islam. This culturalist attitude thus prevents the effective history of the constitution of methods and knowledges in the Muslim world being genuinely grasped, and, in particular, that of their transmission to Europe.[164]

To return to Al Afghânî's response to Renan, we can also understand its nature by pointing out that the more complete reply he could have made was in fact elsewhere than in his brief contribution to a debate conducted in a language he was not proficient in. Its expression can be found, for example, in a text where he recalls the 'utility of philosophy', which allowed the Islamic world to open up to science by being able to take lessons from peoples under its domination by translating the works they held. Comparing this attitude to the present state of affairs, he goes on to truly scold the 'scholars of India' to rouse them from the dogmatic slumber into which their ignorance of modern science and its achievements has plunged them:

> look, he basically tells them, at telegraph lines, phonographs, photographs, microscopes…, and update, not your religion, but your understanding of it: 'Is it not incumbent upon you to serve those who will follow you with your highest thoughts, just as your revered predecessors served you? … Is it not a fault for a percipient sage not to learn the entire sphere of new sciences and inventions and fresh creations, when he has no information about their causes and reasons? And when the world has changed from a state to another and he does not raise his hand from the sleep of neglect?[165]

And since Renan spoke in terms of essence, we have there the true essence, for Al Afghânî, of a religion that assigned no limit to the investigation of the nature of things except the de facto limits encountered by rational curiosity itself in its journey of understanding the world.

All of Muhammad Iqbal's statements regarding the scientific spirit of inquiry and analysis are continuous with this line of thinking and aim to reveal the spirit of investigation to itself once again by rediscovering the meaning of the Quranic conception that invites us to think in terms of unlimited life and movement, which he calls, for this reason, 'non-classical'.

On the notion of limit, Iqbal asserts of thought that it is 'in its essential nature, incapable of limitation … In the wide world beyond itself nothing is alien to it. It is in its progressive participation in the life of the apparently alien that thought demolishes the walls of its finitude and enjoys its potential infinitude.' And he goes on to point out that the refusal of limits belongs, so to speak, to the very principle of thought, since its impetus is precisely to be tormented by the infinite; thus, as has already been mentioned, the infinite is not only offered to its activity, from the outside, but is encountered, living within thought as the principle of its deployment: 'Its movement becomes possible only because of the implicit presence in its finite individuality of the infinite, which keeps alive within it the flame of aspiration and sustains its endless pursuit'.[166]

As for the classical or anti-classical character of the Quranic conception, it indicates the necessity for Iqbal to find this genuine spirit of the Quran and to make a break with the spirit of Greek philosophy; he writes, in effect, that if the introduction of this philosophy into the spiritual universe of Islam undoubtedly represented an opening for Muslim thinkers, it nevertheless succeeded in clouding a reading of the Quran that he believes should be reconstructed today.

Transposed to the pointed and brusque language of poetry, this thesis translates into formulas that suggest a rupture with the approach of the Hellenizing *falâsifa* like Al Farâbî (died 950) and first of all with the master of them all, the divine Plato himself. Thus the seventh song of *The Secrets of the Self* begins with these lines:

'Plato, the prime ascetic and sage,
Was one of that ancient flock of sheep'.[167]

And the rest of the poem tells us what a strange flock it is a question of: one of 'dead spirits' to whom 'the world of Ideas' is dear, whereas for the 'living spirit' it is the 'world of phenomena' that is sweet. In other words, it is Platonic idealism that is targeted here, as resting, according to the poet, on such a fascination for the 'invisible' that it 'made hand, eye, and ear of no account', which are the true instruments of scientific intelligence, *inductive reasoning*.

In this break then, what is sought by Muhammad Iqbal, more than a critique of the *falsafa*, is in fact, once again, a *reconstruction*: that of an attitude toward the world and toward matter composed from a sense of the concrete in its approach to reality and of inductive reasoning in its approach to acquiring knowledge of it. This approach is the true Quranic spirit, when it is not clouded by the reading that a speculative and deductive philosophy can make of it.

The very general character of this 'disqualification' of the *falsafa* and the Greek philosophy from which it was constituted shows that a *critical* concern – which would aim to present the 'true Plato' and specify the real influences of his thought – is not the primary issue here. In the presentation of *The Development of Metaphysics in Persia*, the concern for accuracy and nuance is real, in virtue of its context of course, even if in this work there is also general support for the idea that there is a concrete thought that can be erected against a Greek philosophy that is essentially speculative, deductive, and more turned towards the subject than towards external things. 'With the study of Greek thought', writes Iqbal in this text for example, 'the spirit which was almost lost in the concrete, begins to reflect and realise itself as the arbiter of truth. Subjectivity asserts itself, and endeavours to supplant all outward authority. Such a period, in the intellectual history of a people, must be the epoch of rationalism, scepticism, mysticism, heresy – forms in which the human mind, swayed by the growing force of subjectivity, rejects all external standards of truth'.[168]

As a result, the notion of an anti-classical spirit to be rediscovered, and empirical or naturalist attitude that would be the Quranic conception itself, acquires above all the meaning of a will to promote *for the sake of the present* the scientific spirit, in its most current form, the one under which it is revealed in the methods and procedures of the sciences of today, and which the philosopher considers to be the spirit of induction. It is this spirit that allows the ego not to go, 'as if it were deaf and blind', past the signs of the 'ultimate Reality' such as revealed in nature and such as can, on the one hand, lead it to knowledge of self and of this Reality, and on the other to the mastery of the universe that is part of its destiny.

Regarding the spirit of induction, Muhammad Iqbal points out that it was part of the principle of the important contributions of the Islamic world to the history of the sciences in many areas, through the implementation of the method of observation and experiment which it showed. And Iqbal especially insists on its non-Aristotelian beginnings, to the extent that it originated in what a title of Ibn-i-Taimiyya's called the *Refutation of Logic*. In other terms, it was a question, for this author and for others, against the claims of the *ars demonstrandi* – or the art of arranging propositions deductively once their truth has been established – to be the instrument of knowledge *par excellence*, of implementing an *ars inveniendi*, an art of inventing that would present itself as a new logical *organon*. We know that Descartes also objected to logicism in these terms, in the name of science.

The reference to Ibn-i-Taimiyya assumes moreover another importance regarding the significance of inductive reasoning for Muhammad Iqbal. He stresses especially the break this author made, in the name of the necessity of *ijtihâd*, with the conformism of the Muslim legists of his time: 'The tendency to over-organization by a false reverence of the past as manifested in the legists of Islam in the thirteenth century and later, was contrary to the inner impulse of Islam, and consequently invoked the powerful reaction of Ibn-i-Taimiyya, one of the most indefatigable writers and preachers of Islam, who was born in 1263, five years after the destruction of Baghdad'.[169]

It is thus a matter of reintroducing the very dynamism of social life, or rather of restarting it, like a stopped clock. And we can thus understand that at bottom, beyond its significance as a scientific method, the inductive spirit has above all the value of a principle of movement: *ijtihâd*.

Ijtihâd and Open Society

In the cultural and intellectual history of the Islamic world, the year 1258 appears as a turning point. It is the date of the sack of Baghdad by the Mongols, then the capital of the dynasty of Abbasid caliphs and the centre of the intellectual life of the Islamic world. This event concentrated the fear of this world disintegrating and the shattering of the Community following the weakening of its central power.

The nature of the circumstances brought by the flow of events as well as the sense of threat may thus have led, historically, to such a concern for preservation and fidelity that this was then conceived as a veritable immobilism. Against the force of divergence naturally borne by the effort of interpretation, cohesion had to be put above everything, and this was assumed to depend on a spirit of conformity. No doubt this reaction – which was certainly neither premeditated nor immediate – was inevitable, and Muhammad Iqbal began by recognising all the importance of this imperative of cohesion in the following lines:

> Follow the path of your fathers, that is where unity is found
> Conformity means the coherence of the community.[170]

He later returns to this response offered by the legists of the community to the disturbances, instability and threats of dislocation: that consisting in declaring closed the gates of *ijtihâd*. As understandable as this reaction was then, it was condemned to turn against itself, or rather against its own ends, by thwarting the only effective power against the forces of decay: the indefinitely open process by which a society aims continuously to be equal to its own principle, and whose impetus, ultimately, is the power of innovation which is always the result of 'self-concious individuals' in a position to reveal 'the depth of life'.[171] This is why it is the same thing to understand that Islam posits the end of prophecy and that it marks the birth of inductive intelligence.

In the idea that prophecy is now sealed, we are not to understand simply that the message is now finished, having succeeded in unfurling its significance in its own closure on itself. In this case, the only thing left for man is to be invited to resistance, to what has been called, by Gaston Berger, a 'retrospective stubbornness' so that, *despite* time, *despite* becoming – thus conceived as a threat to being – it may be permitted to him to remain within what has been achieved for him: time, thereby, is *what fidelity is defined against*.

But in remembering that we must not 'speak ill of time, for time is God', that it is thus not the enemy of being, but one of its modalities, we can understand further this idea than of a sealing of prophecy. Its meaning is illuminated by the scene that has marked the history of Islam, between the companions of the Prophet concerning the question of the future, when, faced with the sickness of their master, they had to confront the idea of a world in which he would no longer be physically present to indicate, without any possibility of controversy, how best to act in each new situation. And we know that in what he knew to be his final moments, the Prophet of Islam had the greatest concern for what would have preserved his community, for ever after, from the test presented by time; that it is Umar who then reminded them energetically that the provisions *viatique* were already in place, which could be nothing other than the Quranic word itself.

Muhammad Iqbal sees in this the complete expression of the spirit of reflection and he writes that Umar was 'the first critical and independent mind in Islam who, at the last moments of the Prophet, had the moral courage to utter these remarkable words: 'The Book of God is sufficient for us".[172]

If he finds these words 'remarkable' and if he sees in them the mark of 'moral courage', as well as the sign of a critical and independent mind, it is essentially because it expresses the notion, which precisely establishes the link between *ijtihâd* and inductive reasoning, of a human reason that has become mature, a human judgement henceforth in a position, when it knows how to effectively draw on the Quranic message, which is to say understand it as a living word always in the present, to formulate new responses to the questions that always arise.

These words of Umar thus express the full significance of the end of the prophecy: to seal this is to signal that humanity, in its capacity to examine and reason, has left its state of minority to enter adulthood: 'In Islam prophecy reaches its perfection in discovering the need of its own abolition. This involves the keen perception that life cannot for ever be kept in leading strings; that in order to achieve full self-consciousness man must finally be thrown back on his own resources. The abolition of priesthood and hereditary kingship in Islam, the constant appeal to reason and experience in the Quran, and the emphasis that it lays on Nature and History as sources of human knowledge, are all different aspects of the same idea of finality'.[173]

It is in the very nature of life to be incompletion and opening, and this is why fidelity is not *despite* time: far from being a rigid resistance to movement and becoming, it proves itself in time, in the sense that it both tests itself there and encounters there its own significance. Because finality, for humanity, lies in attaining full consciousness of self, *fidelity lies in movement*. Movement is thus not a distancing of principles and a fatal draining of their initial meaning but a creative deployment of their significance and, in a manner of speaking, their continuous deepening.

This idea that becoming – far from being a loss of being is, on the contrary, creative – is typical of modernist thought and is also encountered in Muhammad Abduh. He thus expresses perfectly what we could call a *historical optimism*, that 'turns us away from an exclusive attachment to the things that come to us from our fathers' and reveals as 'ignorant and limited those who blindly follow the words of the ancestors': as 'the fact of having come before us constitutes neither proof of knowledge nor superiority of mind or reasoning; … ancestors and their descendants are equal in their critical spirit and natural faculties; … the descendants moreover know the events of the past, they have the leisure of meditating on them and weighing the utility of their consequences, all these things were unavailable to the ancestors'.[174]

Against the concept of a Golden Age whose evolution represents a progressive and inexorable loss following a descending scale of generations, this historical optimism of Abduh's finds an echo in the thought of Iqbal in which we read the same refusal to think of being in a nostalgic mode. This conception is therefore at the heart of what he calls a *meliorism*, which is, he says, neither optimism nor pessimism but responsibility and action in the recognition of a growing universe, with the hope of a final victory of man over the forces of corrosion.[175]

Overall, within the Message that declares itself to be essentially inexhaustible, the philosopher sees above all a call, a clearing, an imperative to become that doesn't hold any sociology sacred but commands it to always aim to be equal to its own principle in the indefinite process of continuous self-creation.

It is a matter, for example, of the clear and firmly established principle in the Quranic text of the radical *ontological* equality of man and woman, sharing a humanity identically emerging from a same and single breath; and on the other hand the diverse and varied sociological realities and becomings of cultures gathered by this Text into a single spiritual world, itself open to the world in general. We will thus call *ijtihâd* the interminable movement, with multiple centers, of the according of this principle and these realities.

The question of the status of women is no doubt the one that is at the heart of this general set of problems concerning fidelity and movement. It is the content to be given to the notion of equality between man and woman, rather than its principle, which is absolute, that is the topic of a discussion of Iqbal's of the imperative, as expressed by the Turkish poet Zia, of their equality in divorce and inheritance. His position on these two points is entirely emblematic of the spirit in which the philosopher proposes to conceive an open society, which is to say, to use Karl Popper's terms, 'a society which is not only *open* to reform but anxious to reform itself'.

Thus, on the question of inheritance, he accuses the Turkish poet of ignoring a principle of prudence necessary in the implementation of *ijtihâd*, which is the consideration of all of the elements of the family economy in general at the heart of a given social structure: thus, alongside inheritance, it is also necessary to take into account the dowry system as well as the general organization of the distribution of wealth in order to try to conceive the content of equality in relation to the concept of fairness. Concerning the question of the right to divorce, Iqbal follows the tendency of the poet by producing a reasoning *ad absurdum* starting with a consideration of the specific case of Punjabi women who, in order to rid themselves of an undesirable husband, are obliged, he says, to resort to apostasy: thus it is that a right whose highest aim is to protect the religion leads to its abandonment. We can add here a remark concerning the status of women in general by pointing out that Iqbal is clearly in favor of monogamy even if he sometimes considers that the universalization of this principle should be deferred for prudential reasons: the reasons thus express, in his opinion, society being as it is, the necessity to protect all women by marriage.[176]

Because infidelity is, in the final analysis, in the arrest of the movement that is the very life of the principle, the lesson is this: sociologies must always seek to be adequate to the imperative that founds them and which is placed ahead of them, so to speak. Thus it is that when questioned on the status of women in Islam, Eva de Vitray-Meyerovitch, precisely referring to the philosophy of Iqbal, declared that on this model 'sociologies do not follow'.[177]

We already find in the philosopher Al Farâbi, in the 10th century, this idea that beyond a particular present content that determines human actions, there always remains an indeterminacy that, far from being simply residual, is on the contrary desirable and necessary, because it signifies the ability of a society to always trace its path toward an open future. Thus, for Al Farâbi, to faithfully follow the example of the first lawmaker is also to know how to determine actions differently.[178] Such is the meaning of inductive reasoning for the philosopher: it is the *reasoning* of principles of determination and not simply the *memorizing* of the acts posited using these principles. It is, in an essential way, this freedom, which Iqbal's thought refers back to, of a movement that unhinges tradition (in the sense as well in which we speak of a train, for example, sputtering off) that is clearly expressed in these lines which conclude *The Message from the East*:

> How good it would be for man with a free step
> To go, unfettered by the chains of the past!
> If imitation were a good thing,
> The prophet would himself have also followed
> the path of his forebears.

Conclusion

On Modernity

We cannot fail, after referring so often to the 'modernist' current in which the Iqbalian philosophy is inscribed, to examine the very notion of modernity. Firstly by repeating that Iqbal quite particularly insists on the idea that this cannot be about a particular *content* to imitate. And this refusal as much concerns the imitation of a tradition as an external model. Modernity here is thus not something which it would be a matter of a society conforming to, but, in a manner of speaking, a mirror held out to it.

In a long and important reflection entitled 'Response to questions raised by Pandit J. L. Nehru',[179] Muhammad Iqbal returns to the notion of an appeal to modernity which is the internal movement of a society even if it is also in order to respond to the pressure of modern *ideas*. It is thus that he considers, on the one hand, the personal history of modernist intellectuals in the Islamic world, like Al Afghânî and Sayyid Ahmad Khan, on the other, the transformations in Turkey. Just as, he declares, we cannot say that these intellectuals were Westernized when they were in the first place the outcrop of the old traditional school, we also – and he is responding directly to a statement of Nehru's – cannot say that the modernisation undertaken in Turkey meant that this country had ceased to be Muslim. Whether it is a matter of the necessity of also having a materialist perspective on the world, or other questions such as the use of Turkish language written in Roman characters or the abolition of the caliphate with the separation of Church and State, there is nothing in these, Iqbal says, that cannot be referred, ultimately, to an *internal* principle of movement, to the *ijtihâd* of an Islamic country.[180]

Rather than a particular content that is modern, then, we can refer to an *attitude* of modernity, thus making use of an important and useful distinction employed by Michel Foucault, who specifies: 'by 'attitude', I mean a mode of relating to contemporary reality; a voluntary choice made by certain people; in the end, a way of thinking and feeling; a way, too, of acting and behaving that at one and the same time marks a relation of belonging and presents itself as a task. No doubt, a bit like what the Greeks called an *ethos*'.[181]

An *ethos* that is both belonging and task, such indeed is the principle that is at work in modernist thought and that can be defined using the illustration he finds in Amir Ali's conclusions concerning the status of women in the Islamic world. When the author of the *Spirit of Islam* indicates that, on this issue, Islamic societies must move with the advances of civilisation, it is not an appeal to conform with civilisation or with modernity. It is by knowing how to go back to Islamic history and to the *process of civilisation* that it bears in order to constitute, in the present and for this time, its *sense*, which is to say the direction it indicates.

It is a matter of going against a static, because purely reactionary and defensive, use of History, perfectly captured by the expression *retrospective stubbornness*: the use that consists in devoting all considerations of the status of women in Islam – and thereby by blocking it – to recapitulating the advances, considerable in effect, that the appearance of this religion represented, on every level, for those whose ontological equality with men, once again, had been clearly posited. The whole direction of Amir Ali's approach is to substitute for this rigid use what can be called a 'dynamic constitution of history' which is not satisfied with establishing the observation of what progress the condition of women has known, but to read in this progress an *intention* which then becomes imperative to *pursue*.[182] And already, he observes, as has already been mentioned, the Mu'tazilite school of theology proceeded in this spirit.

We can thus see in the attitude of modernity the imperative for a reading of history that would reconstitute its intention, according to the conditions and demands of the present and with the end of continuing to open the future by always further increasing the freedom of each and all. It is this attitude, expressed with the greatest philosophical clarity in Muhammad Iqbal's work, which is at the foundation of the great constitutive themes of modernist Islamic thought, such as can be read in its different representatives: the necessity of promoting the capacity of judging for oneself by making use of reason, reason as a faculty allowing man to pursue the intention of religion which only in this way can address the whole of humanity, since thanks to reason the temporary can be distinguished from the permanent, the universal from the particular, etc.

In many respects, the Indian sub-continent has been the place of emergence, for the modern era, of this principle. Richard Khuri thus points out that it is after Shah Wali-ullah (1702–1763) that 'Islamic intellectuals learned to make the distinction between the eternal *principles* of the Quran and the specific *injunctions* derived from these, most of these latter being inscribed within the limits of the temporal'.[183]

Modernist thinkers share the observation that Islamic societies have come to stagnate as a result of a state of juridical petrification, a dogmatic rigidity regarding doctrines whose authors had nevertheless always declared that they were simply possible ways of seeing things. Historians thus remind us that the founders of the four main schools of jurisprudence, Hanafism (from the name of its first teacher, Abû Hanifa, died 767), Malikism (from Malik ibn Anas, died 795), Shafi'ism (from Ash-Shâfi, died 820) and Hanbalism (from Ahmad ibn Hanbal, died 855) were extremely careful not to fix the result of their work and research as dogma or sole point of reference. And Ash-Shâfi, when he left Iraq to settle in Egypt, also set about proposing different answers to the questions he had posed.

The point of departure for Iqbal's reflection on the 'principle of movement in Islam' could thus be Amir Ali's remark on the 'current stagnation of Islamic communities, mainly due, according to this author, to the idea that has become fixed in the minds of Muslims as a group, that the exercise of individual judgement stopped with the first legists, that this exercise in modern times is a sin. A Muslim who wants to be considered as an orthodox follower of the path of the prophet should necessarily belong to one or other of the juridical paths established by the Islamic school founders and abandon his whole ability to judge, in an absolute manner, to the interpretation of men who lived in the 9th century and who could in absolutely no way imagine the necessities of the 20th'.[184] Following this observation, Amir Ali mentions, as Iqbal will also, evoking the attitude of the Caliph Umar, that those who think in this way in a spirit of completion and closure of meaning 'have forgotten that the prophet ... addressed himself to the whole of humanity' and that he thus 'sanctioned reason as the highest and most noble function of the human intellect', the one 'the school founders and those who follow them servilely have declared that its exercise is a sin and a crime!'[185]

We could think that, even when Islamic faith has reached as far as the Inuit world, the correct procedure to follow is for it still to be expressed using the rules of jurisprudence that have been developed for the conduct of the Iraqis, to use an example given by Amir Ali.[186] And can we not see that to question such a state of affairs is not inspired by a relativistic position but, on the contrary, by the very concern for universality. The principle of modernity, which conjugates fidelity and movement, is precisely what allows us to declare, following Pascal's eloquent formula, that we can affirm the opposite of what the Ancients said, without contradicting them; 'even if we are led to differ from those who preceded us', Iqbal has written in the same spirit.[187]

Everything occurs as if what the 'Fathers' established thereafter stood in all its thickness between the Islamic societies of today and what they should remain faithful to. As if a religion with no Church in principle had in the end taken on the burden of the heaviest patristics. Hence this idea that the 'religious invention of modernity', that 'major modality in the history of the West',[188] today requires, in order to reconcile fidelity with movement, that the Islamic schools accomplish the Reformation that consists in freeing the spirit of all the accumulated weight from centuries of a strictly literal reading whose principle was above all conformity.

For Muhammad Iqbal as well, the period that Islamic societies are moving through is entirely similar to the one that finally led to the Protestant Revolution in Europe and requires that these societies well understand the lesson of the movement instigated by Luther. It is, in analogous fashion, a matter of shaking off the weight of a scholasticism that has itself gone against the intentions of the school founders in order to 're-interpret the foundational legal principles, in the light of ... experience and the altered conditions of modern life'.[189]

It is thus the spirit of the Reformation that Iqbal calls on when he speaks of 'stirring into activity the dormant spirit of life in our legal system', or when at the end of the last of his *Lectures*, he invites his audience to leave behind 'that intellectual laziness which, especially in the period of spiritual decay, turns great thinkers into idols'.[190]

If the task ahead is conceived on the model of the European Reformation, Iqbal is highly aware that one of the consequences of this religious revolution was a plurality of *churches* where it had been a matter of restoring the *Church*. This is another lesson to draw from the Reformation. He goes so far as to say that the national ethical systems that had progressively displaced the universal Christian ethic are those that confronted each other during the Great War that tore Europe apart.[191] This comment of Iqbal's is aligned with the reflections of the theologian Ernst Troeltsch (1865–1923) concerning the real relationship between Protestantism and progress. He recalls that in effect only the illusion of hindsight can give any credence to the idea that the aim of the Reformation was, in any conscious way, what we call modernity. On the contrary, the Protestant goal of reforming the Church in its totality saw itself deviated toward the constitution of its own churches which only then became 'national', he says, 'simply because Protestantism could only realise its ideal of the Church with the aid of governmental authority, and therefore had to be content not to apply it beyond the national frontiers'.[192]

But, once again, beyond the question of particular contents, remains the *ethos*, the imperative. And at the basis of this imperative, we find the key Iqbalian concepts that are inter-connected within his philosophy of action: the cosmological concept of the incompletion of the world and the ethical concept of human responsibility. Upon reflection then, and even if pluralism and difference represent a test – but life is test – the movement of the Reformation is, or should be, the very spirit of Islam since the Quranic conception of life is one of a process of continuous creation, of permanent innovation and emergence, which prevent the intention of religion becoming imprisoned within reasonings and legal interpretations claiming a 'final character'. And it is also for this reason that human responsibility is also generational, in other words that it belongs to each generation to rise to its own responsibility of rethinking the legal principles in function of its own problems and thus in always aiming to return Islamic thought to its first movement.

Notes

1. Sayyid Amir Ali, *The Spirit of Islam: A History of the Evolution and Ideals of Islam with a Life of the Prophet,* London: Christophers, 1922:349. Henceforth this title will simply be referred to as *The Spirit of Islam.* The 'House' refers to the family of the prophet of Islam and its direct descendents.

2. *Spirit of Islam,* p. 232.

3. Muhammad Iqbal, *The Mysteries of Selflessness: A Philosophical Poem,* English translation from the Persian by Arthur J. Arberry (available online at the Iqbal Academy Pakistan site: http://www.allamaiqbal.com/), originally published in 1918 to follow the 1915 work *The Secrets of Self,* together representing Iqbal's decision to write a philosophical poetry.

4. ASRAR-I-KHUDI: *The Secrets of the Self,* trans. into English from the Persian by Reynold A. Nicholson (available online at the Iqbal Academy Pakistan site: http://www.allamaiqbal.com/), Prologue, line 12.

5. *The Secrets of the Self,* line 33 & 34.

6. *The Mysteries of Selflessness,* 'The Author's Memorial to Him Who is a Mercy to All Living Beings'.

7. From the Introduction to Djamchid Mortazavi and Eva de Vitray-Meyerovitch's translation into French of *The Secrets of the Self* followed by *The Mysteries of Selflessness (Les secrets du soi suivi par les mystères du non-moi,* Paris: Albin Michel, 1989), p. 7. In a book of interviews with Rachel and Jean-Paul Cartier entitled *Islam, l'autre visage* ('Islam, the other face', Paris: Albin Michel, 1991), Eva de Vitray-Meyerovitch talks about the profound resonance Iqbal's thought had in her own spiritual life and which led her to adopt the Islamic faith. In any case, Iqbal's work has found in her a translator that allows the Francophone reader to savor all of the beauty of his poetry. Elsewhere, in their *Panorama de la pensée islamique (Panorama of Islamic Thought,* Paris: Editions Sinbad, 1984), Sheikh Bouamrane and Louis Gardet say of Iqbal that this 'source of inspiration and meditation for the young people, scholars and politicians of today and tomorrow … is perhaps the greatest Islamic scholar of the 14th century of hijra, when his range of knowledges, his breadth of mind and the courage of his positions is taken into account', pp. 310-311.

8. The date 22 February 1873 is given by his biographer Sheikh Abdul Qadir, who knew him as a student, at the end of the 19th century and stayed his friend throughout his life. This date has often been used by many commentators. But Muhammad Hanif Shahid, who edited Sheikh Abdul Qadir's recollections under the title *Iqbal the Great Poet of Islam* (Lahore, 1975), indicates in this work that the research undertaken to determine the exact date of birth of the philosopher poet

led to that of '3, Ziqaad 1294 A.H', given by Muhammad Iqbal himself, and corresponding to 9 November 1877. The biographical elements found here are drawn from this work by Sheikh Abdul Qadir.

9. Later to become Iqbal College.

10. It is also important to mention in his regard that he shared the ideas of Sayyid Ahmad Khan (1817-1898), who stressed the need for Muslims to firstly emerge from their state of intellectual backwardness through education. In 1875 he founded Aligarh College, which in 1922 became a university and was a place of propagation of his own modernist ideas. We learn from Lini S. May (*Iqbal. His Life and Times*, Lahore, 1974, p. 52) that Mîr Hasan inculcated his disciple Iqbal with the following doctrine: "divine unity, human unity", and that it signified, on the political level among others, the need for a unity between Hindu and Muslim Indians against the separatist forces within each community.

11. *Iqbal the Great Poet of Islam*, p. 71.

12. Ibid., p. 72.

13. Ibid., p. 27.

14. Eva de Vitray-Meyerovitch has translated this work into French under the title *La métaphysique en Perse* (Paris: Sinbad, 1980).

15. From *Iqbal, the Poet of Tomorrow*, Khawaja Abdur Rahim, Lahore 1968:7. These are the proceedings of a symposium dedicated to Iqbal in Lahore in 1963. Dagh (1831-1905) was a grand master of Urdu poetry to whom Iqbal had sent his poems in order to receive his comments. Regarding the ghazal poetic form, Eva de Vitray-Meyerovitch writes: 'It was originally always a poem of profane love, then it often came to take on a mystical meaning. The ghazal, which always has a particularly deliberate form, is based on a single rhyme, comprising a certain unity of inspiration, but each line is independent and complete in itself and does not directly follow on from the idea expressed in the preceding line'. (from the Introduction to *Le Message de l'Orient*, a collection of writings by Iqbal translated by Eva de Vitray-Meyerovitch with Mohammed Achena, Paris: Les Belles Lettres, 1956:17.

16. Ibid.

17. Ibid., p. 9.

18. Ibid., p. 11. Towards the end of his life he will write in Urdu again, on the themes of his philosophical poetry in Persian, especially under pressure, as Sheikh Abdul Qadir indicates, from his admirers who wanted to see him contribute, once more, to the literature in this language, *Iqbal the Great Poet of Islam*, p. 112. Furthermore concerning Iqbal's decision to write in Persian, Abdul Qadir attributes a rather contingent reason to it by telling an anecdote according to which during a dinner with friends in London, Iqbal was questioned as to his ultimate ability to write poetry in this language. His response, Abdul Qadir says, was two ghazals in Persian 'that he showed him the next morning', ibid., p. 73.

19. The kingdom of God on earth, he replied to a critic who thought Iqbal could be reproached with thinking that only Muslims would be entitled to this, belongs to all men 'provided they renounce the idols of race and nationality and treat each other as personalities' (my emphasis: this statement is cited in Riaz Hussain, *The Politics of Iqbal*, Lahore, 1977:26). Generally speaking, Iqbal's philosophy could not be further from the compartmentalisation of identity politics: 'Break all the

idols of tribe and caste,/Break the ancient customs that keep men in chains!', he writes in *The Wing of Gabriel,* cited in *Mohammad Iqbal* by Luce-Claude Maitre, Paris: P. Seghers, 1964:135. The notion, which is central in his philosophy, of personality places identity within the affirmation, within the movement – which is life itself – of an ego tending always further toward more freedom of self-creation and not in the belonging that thereby constitutes a negation of identity, cf. below the Chapter entitled 'A Politics of Autonomy'.

20. From Abdur Rahim, *The Poet of Tomorrow,* p. 5.

21. French translation: *Reconstruire la pensée religieuse de l'islam,* trans. Eva de Vitray-Meyerovitch, Paris: Maisonneuve, 1955. These lectures took place in the universities of Aligarh, Hyderabad and Madras. Iqbal later added a chapter at the time of publication.

22. In his Presentation of the *Dîwân de Halladj,* Paris: Seuil, 1981:18.

23. Sir Mohammad Iqbal, *The Reconstruction of Religious Thought in Islam,* London, Humphrey Milford: Oxford University Press, 1934:104. References to this work concern this edition and will sometimes simply be referred to as the *Lectures.*

24. Ibid., p. 4.

25. Op. cit. (*Dîwân de Halladj*), p. 84. Regarding Abû Yazîd al Bistâmî (d. 874), G. C. Anawati and Louis Gardet write, in *Mystique musulmane. Aspects et tendances expériences et techniques,* Paris: Vrin, 1986, 4th ed., that his aim was 'aloneness before the pure divine Essence – without however espousing the "monism of being", despite the interpretation that Ibn Arabi was to give to this'; and they go on to cite this statement of the Sufi: 'I shedded my Self as a snake sheds its skin; then I considered my essence: and I was, me, Him', p. 32.

26. Which can be summarized very generally by saying that for such a philosophy beings proceed from the One by a process of the emanation of its essence; a notion to which is necessarily linked that of a hierarchy of beings, an ontological gradation where the quality of being will depend on rank, i.e. proximity to the Source.

27. *Reconstruction,* p. 106. The reference to Renan concerns the following statement: 'A living and permanent humanity, such thus seems to be the meaning of the Averroistic theory of the unity of the intellect. The immortality of the active intellect is thus nothing other than the eternal rebirth of humanity and the perpetuity of civilization'. Ernest Renan, *Averroès et l'averroïsme,* Paris: Maisonneuve et Larose, 1997:109. The first edition of this book dates from 1852.

28. *The Development of Metaphysics in Persia: A Contribution to the History of Muslim Philosophy,* by Muhammad Iqbal, London: Luzac and Company, 1908:148.

29. *Metaphysics in Persia,* p. 93.

30. *Metaphysics in Persia,* p. 113. When presenting the Sheikh Shahâb Al-Dîn Suhrawardî (1155-1191), Iqbal mentions that the dogmatic theologians had him sentenced to death at 36—for this reason he has the nickname *al Maqtûl,* 'the slain'—and draws from this the following double lesson: on the one hand that dogmatism, 'conscious of its inherent weakness, has always managed to keep brute force behind its back', p. 96; on the other hand that 'Murderers have passed away, but the philosophy, the price of which was paid in blood, still lives, and attracts many an earnest seeker after truth', p. 97.

31. If two objects in the world were identical, it would contravene the principle of sufficient reason that their situation be different and thus able to be distinguished. Consequently, there can be no two objects that are perfectly the same.

32. Regarding souls, which he considers to be like 'incorporel lights', Suhrawardi declares that 'they are distinguished intelligibly through their cognizance of themselves, through their cognizance of their Lights and the illuminations of their lights and through a particularity based on their control of the fortress'. *The philosophy of illumination*, English translation by John Walbridge and Hossein Ziai, Provo, UT: Brigham Young University Press, 1999:§243, p.148. The term 'fortress' here is a metaphor for the body.

33. *Metaphysics in Persia*, Iqbal considers that this new philosophical attitude, which he holds responsible for 'the progress of recent political reform in Persia', has been encouraged by the religious movement known under the name of Babism, p.149.

34. *Reconstruction*, p. 187.

35. From the version given at the end of *Reconstruction*, p. 187.

36. *The Secrets of the Self*, line 241.

37. *Javid Nama*, line 2405-2406.

38. *Reconstruction*, in the Preface written by Louis Massignon for the French translation of this work, he indicates that the figure of Hallaj, often associated with Nietzsche, was one of the themes of his exchanges with Iqbal who, he says, saw in him 'one who, beyond ecstasy, manifested and expressed the supreme defiance of personalism'. *Reconstruire la pensée religieuse de l'islam*, trans, p.91. Eva de Vitray-Meyerovitch, Paris: Maisonneuve, 1955:4, my emphasis. He indicates that this reading of Hallaj's theopathic words makes these, in the eyes of his friend Iqbal, a 'personalist testimony from a divine rebel'.

39. *Secrets of the Self*, line 850.

40. *L'Aile de Gabriel*, trans. from Urdu by Mirza Saïd-Uz-Zafar Chaghtaï and Suzanne Bussac, Paris: Albin Michel, 1977:107.

41. *L'Aile de Gabriel*, p. 111.

42. *Message from the East*, versified English translation from the Persian by M. Hadi Hussain available online at the Iqbal Academy Pakistan site: http://www.allamaiqbal.com/. This collection of Iqbal's poetry is presented by its author as an echo of the *East-West Divan (Westöstlicher Diwan)* that Goethe wrote between 1814 and 1819 in the tradition of Eastern poetry.

43. English Ref.

44. *Reconstruction*, p. 60.

45. *Reconstruction*, p. 60.

46. Quran sura 112, English trans. M. Asad.

47. Henri Bergson, *Creative Evolution*, trans. into English by Arthur Mitchell, New York: Henry Holt and Company, 1911:13.

48. *Reconstruction*, p. 59.

49. Gaston Berger, 'Le temps et la participation dans l'oeuvre de Louis Lavelle', *Phénoménologie du temps et prospective*, Paris: Presses Universitaires de France, 1964: 177.

50. Cf. *Reconstruction*, p. 57.

51. *Reconstruction*, p. 57.

52. Richard K. Khuri, who has devoted an important work to the notions of openness and freedom in Islam, has written highly elucidating pages on Iqbal's philosophy, in which, regarding this question of time, he opposes the analytic mode of the intellect to what he calls an appreciative mode, *Freedom, Modernity and Islam. Toward a Creative Synthesis*, Syracuse: Syracuse University Press, 1998:322. Those familiar with Gaston Berger will perhaps see in this notion of an 'appreciative' mode what this author calls a prospective attitude based on "a phenomenology of time" which is itself an 'indispensable introduction to a metaphysics of Eternity'. And, in fact, for Berger, 'after the phenomenological reduction, there isn't any time, there is the present'. See Berger, *Phenomenologie du temps et prospective*, p. 252 and p. 131.

53. *Reconstruction*, p. 29. Iqbal examines the Cosmological, Teleological and Ontological arguments in the second *Lecture* devoted to the 'The Philosophical Test of the Revelations of Religious Experience'.

54. *Reconstruction*, pp. 5-6.

55. *Reconstruction*, p. 6.

56. Translated into English by Michael E. Marmura, Provo: Brigham Young University Press, 1997.

57. Al-Ghazâlî, *The Incoherence of the Philosophers*, p. 12.

58. *Reconstruction*, p. 62.

59. Ibid., p. 99.

60. Ibid., p. 100.

61. Ibid., p. 100-101.

62. Ibid., p. 100.

63. Ibid., p. 53-54. M. S. Raschid, who has devoted an extremely critical work to Iqbal's thought *Iqbal's Concept of God*, London and Boston: Kegan Paul International, 1981, refuses there this reading: this 'custom' of God only applies to human matters and society, he believes should be offered as an alternative reading, to 'save' the divine from immanence.

64. *Reconstruction*, p. 62.

65. Ibid., p. 52.

66. Ibid., p. 57.

67. Ibid., p. 57.

68. *Secrets of the Self*, lines 213-214.

69. *Reconstruction*, p. 44. In a letter written in 1931 and addressed to Sir William Rothenstein, Iqbal tells the story of his meeting with Bergson in Paris. Although he was very old and sick, he writes, Bergson was kind enough to make an exception to his prohibition of visitors to receive him and talk with him, for two hours, on philosophical topics, Berkeley among others. And Iqbal adds that, unfortunately, the friend who had taken notes during this interview was later incapable of deciphering his own handwriting, *Letters and Writings of Iqbal*, Karachi: Iqbal Academy, 1967:103.

70. *Creative Evolution*, p. 2.

71. *Reconstruction,* p. 45.

72. *Ibid.,* p. 47.

73. Ibid., p. 50.

74. Ibid., p. 52.

75. *Phénoménologie*, p. 271.

76. Ibid., p. 232.

77. Ibid., p. 235.

78. *Reconstruction*, p. 53, p. 58.

79. Ibid., p. 53.

80. Ibid., p. ?.

81. *Message from the East.*

82. *Message from the East*, 'The Conquest of Nature'.

83. *Message from the East*, 'The Conquest of Nature'.

84. *Message from the East*, 'The Conquest of Nature'?.

85. *Secrets of the Self,* Nicholson translation and introduction reproduced on the Iqbal Academy Pakistan site: http://www.allamaiqbal.com/.

86. *Reconstruction*, pp. 103-104.

87. Ibid., p. 104.

88. Javid Nama, 'Zinda-Rud Propounds his Problems to the Great Spirits', line 2246.

89. Javid Nama, 'Zinda-Rud Propounds his Problems to the Great Spirits', lines 2251-54.

90. *L'aide de Gabriel*, #33, p.64. We also find the following translation by Naeem Sidiqqi:

Raise thy Selfhood so high that before each dispensation,
God Himself may ask thee what thy wishes are.

91. Javid Nama, 'Zinda-Rud Propounds his Problems to the Great Spirits', lines 2231-2234.

92. *Reconstruction*, p. 103. This distinction made between two opposed ways of understanding and living the feeling of fate corresponds to that which exists between the 'words taqdîr and quismat' to express destiny: the first implies the sense of power, of ability, which is that of the verb qadara; in the second there is the idea of division, of splitting, and thus of the lot or share that falls to us and that we receive. 'No quismat', Iqbal writes, marking a subheading of a work he aimed to write *Letters and Writings of Iqbal*, p. 107.

93. *Gabriel's Wing*, French p. 107.

94. *Reconstruction*, p.103. There is nothing incomprehensibly mystical in this significance of prayer, Iqbal explains: "Prayer as a means of spiritual illumination is a normal vital act by which the little island of our personality suddenly discovers its situation in a larger whole of life", *Reconstruction*, p. 85.

95. *Reconstruction*, pp. 88-89.

96. Cheikh Hamidou Kane, *L'aventure ambiguë*, Paris: UGE, 1961; English trans. *Ambiguous Adventure,* by Katherine Walker, New York: Walker and Company, 1963, p.100.

97. *Message de l'Orient*, p.142.

98. Edgar Morin, *Amour poésie sagesse*, Paris: Seuil, 1997:69. 'Life', Iqbal writes, 'is simply inner fire!', *Gabriel's Wing*, French ref. p. 59.

99. *The Poet of Tomorrow*, p. 15. We find here one of the meanings of the philosophical tale of Farîd uddîn Attar, the Sufi poet, *The Conference of the Birds*; at the end of the quest, it is indeed what they are, themselves, that is encountered by the birds who go in search of the fabulous Being that is the ultimate object of all dreams.

100. *Gabriel's Wing*, #24. The Zarathustra of Nietzsche, whose figure if not thought is very present, as is known, in Iqbal's work, similarly says that the richest man can live alone in a cottage without losing a single fraction of his wealth. We can furthermore recall, still in relation to Nietzsche, the pleasure of difference stressed by Gilles Deleuze in *Nietzsche et la philosophie* (Paris: Presses Universitaires de France, 1962, p. 10; English translation *Nietzsche and Philosophy* by Hugh Tomlinson, London: Athlone Press, 1983, p. 9): "What a will wants is to affirm its difference. In its essential relation with the 'other' a will makes its difference an object of affirmation. 'The pleasure of knowing oneself different', the enjoyment of difference; this is the new, aggressive and elevated conceptual element…".

101. *Message from the East*, 'The Glow-Worm'.

102. There is also this dialogue between the firefly and the moth (French ref. p. 98):

    The moth:

      – The firefly is far from being equal to the moth

      What is to boast about a fire with no heat?

    The firefly:

      – I thank God a thousand times that I am not a moth.

      I would never beg fire from others!

103. Cited in *Reconstruction*, pp. 112-113.

104. *Reconstruction*, p. 113.

105. *Message from the East*, French ref. p. 157. This theme runs throughout the whole of Iqbal's poetic work. Thus we find again these lines in the Persian psalms:

    Do not aspire to the end of the journey as you have no end,
    As soon as you touch the goal, you lose your soul.
    Do not think we are ripe, we are raw material,
    For each destination, we are perfect and imperfect.
    Never reach the goal: that's what it is to live!
    (in Luce-Claude Maitre, *Mohammad Iqbal*, p. 125).

106. Cited in *Reconstruction*, p. 115. The convergence of perspectives between Iqbal and Pierre Teilhard de Chardin has often been evoked. Eva de Vitray-Meyerovitch points out that they knew each other (in *Islam, l'autre visage*, Paris: Albin Michel, 1991, p. 37). But the true meeting, for Iqbal, is with Rûmî.

107. *Message from the East*, French ref: pp. 120-121.

108. *Reconstruction*, p. 117.

109. *Reconstruction*, p. 116, p. 117.

110. Cf. for example Sayyid Amir Ali who, in Chapter III of *The Spirit of Islam*, precisely devoted to "the idea of future life in Islam", makes an effort to respond to those who refer to its sensual character by spiritualizing the parabolic description of this future life.

111. *Reconstruction*, pp. 106-107.

112. Pierre Teilhard de Chardin, *Le milieu divin*, Paris: Seuil, 1957:39-40. English trans. *The Divine Milieu* by Sion Cowell, Sussex Academic Press, 2004:18.

113. It seems unjust moreover to make the Nietzschean overman into the return, hopelessly identical, of an already infinitely repeated combination. In fact, and Deleuze insists on this point, the eternal return is creative and agrees in this sense with the Iqbalian doctrine of the achievement/invention of the world by the perfect man.

114. *Javid Nama*, 'The Station of the German Philosopher Nietzsche'. This cry of Nietzsche/Hallaj thus forms an echo to Satan's quest, he also, as we have seen, being in search of Man.

115. *Javid Nama*, 'Song of the Angels'. Cf also Luce-Claude Maître's Introduction to *Mohammad Iqbal*, in particular, p. 70, the recalling of the Quranic nature of the Iqbalian idea of the overman.

116. *Javid Nama*, French ref. p. 63.

117. Anwarul Haq: 'Iqbal's Conception of the Human Ego', in *Iqbal, the Poet of Tomorrow*, p. 74. The passage by Javid Iqbal alluded to is found in the same volume, p. 15, in an article entitled 'Introduction to the Study of Iqbal'. *Faqr* is an Arabic word meaning 'poverty'. Kasb-hilal is, literally, the fact of acquiring (earning one's livelihood by) licit goods.

118. *The Mysteries of Selflessness*, under the title: "That Despair, Grief, and Fear are the Mother of Abominations, Destroying Life and the Belief in the Unity of God puts an end to those Foul Diseases.

119. Thus, for example, despising the limited world of the partridges, the falcon sings:

> *My blue sky is limitless!*
> *I am the dervish of the world of birds*
> *As the falcon builds no nest.*
> (*L'aile de Gabriel's*, p. 130).

And in order to denounce the petrification of movement represented by the idea that one can hold a 'marabout's seat' simply by inheritance, it is quite naturally in the language of the birds that he declares: 'The crows have monopolized the eagles' nests', ibid.

120. Cited by Luce-Claude Maître, p. 38. The poet often insists on this point. Thus he returns to the theme in these lines:

> You are not yet liberated from the bonds of water and clay,
> You say that you are Afghan, or else Turkish;
> Me, I am first of all a man, without mark or color:
> I am only afterwards Indian or Turanian.
> *Message de l'Orient*, p. 81.

121. *L'aile de Gabriel*, p. 122.

122. *Message de l'Orient*, p. 153.

123. *L'aile de Gabriel*, p. 56.

124. Hélène Cixous, *L'Indiade ou l'Inde de leurs rêves*, Paris: Théâtre du Soleil, 1987.

125. *Letters of Iqbal to Jinnah*, Lahore, 1963.

126. Cited in *Iqbal, the Poet of Tomorrow*, p. 21.

127. Cf. p. 58, *Letters and Writings of Iqbal*, compiled and edited by B. A. Dar, Karachi: Iqbal Academy, 1967.

128. Saleem M. M. Qureshi writes in *Jinnah and the Making of a Nation*, Karachi, 1969:9-10, that: 'the significance of the year 1926 lies in the rupture, which came after many separations followed by reunions, which ended the Hindu-Islamic honeymoon whose first phase of life was that of the Khalifat Movement'.

129. Cited by Javid Iqbal in 'Introduction to the Study of Iqbal', p. 16.

130. Jawaharlal Nehru, *The Discovery of India*, New York:The John Day Company, 1946.

131. This recollection on Iqbal and the idea of Pakistan is found, pp. 354-355 of the cited work.

132. Lini S. May, *Iqbal, His Life and Times*, Lahore, 1974.

133. Cited in Sharif Al Mujahid, *Quaid-i-Azam Jinnah: Studies in Interpretation*, Karachi: Quaid-i-Azam Academy, 1981.

134. See Lini S. May, *Iqbal, His Life and Times*, p. 245.

135. The text of the speech – 'Presidential Address Delivered at the Annual Session of the All-India Muslim League at Allahabad on the 29th December 1930' – can be found in *Speeches and Statements of Iqbal*, compiled by A. R. Tariq, Lahore, 1973:3-32.

136. *The Illusion of Cultural Identity*, English translation by Steven Rendall, Janet Roitman, Cynthia Schoch, and Jonathan Derrick, Chicago: The University of Chicago Press, 2005.

137. *The Illusion of Cultural Identity*, p. 87.

138. Cf. Saleem M. M. Qureshi, *Jinnah and the Making of a Nation*, p. 18.

139. *The Illusion of Cultural Identity*, pp. 86-87.

140. This letter dated 28 March 1909 is cited by Lini S. May in *Iqbal, His Life and Times*, p.79. The emphasis in this passage is Iqbal's.

141. Cf. *Speeches and Statements of Iqbal*, p. 10. The observation made by Jawaharlal Nehru, in the reflections he wrote between 1942 and 1945, should be noted in parallel. A Muslim middle class did not develop quickly enough in India, he notes. Once there is a generational gap, he writes, in the respective formations of Hindu and Muslim middle classes, which manifests itself on the economical and political levels among others, this produces a psychology of fear in the Muslim group. Cf. *The Discovery of India*, p. 354.

142. *Speeches and Statements*, p. 11.

143. *Speeches and Statements*, p. 14.

144. *Message from the East*, French ref. p. 191.

145. *Reconstruction*, p. 151 and 154. It should however be mentioned that on many points Muhammad Iqbal discusses the 'poet's Ijtihad' which, he says, 'is open to grave objections' (p. 153). The poet in question is Khâlid Zia Uçaglil (1866-1945).

146. The plan of the projected work can be found in *Letters and Writings of Iqbal*, pp.86-95.

147. *Letters and Writings*, p. 86.

148. *Letters and Writings*, p. 172.

149. Majid Fakhry, *A History of Islamic Philosophy* (New York: Columbia University Press, 1970).

150. Muhammad Abduh French: Rissâlat al Tawhîd or *Exposé de la religion musulmane*, trans. B. Michel and Cheikh Moustapha Abdel Razik (Paris: Librairie orientaliste Paul Geuthner, 1984).

151. *Exposé de la religion musulmane*, p. 107.

152. *Exposé de la religion musulmane*, p. 109.

153. Fakhry, *A History of Islamic Philosophy*, p. 355.

154 .Thus, for example, we find in the collection *Les religions d'Abraham et la science* (Maisonneuve et Larose, 1996) a text entitled 'Islam and Science: The Interpretation of a Geologist' (by E. Hilmy), whose position illustrates this kind of approach: we thus read there that when the Quranic text gives, among the images that represent the day of Judgement, one of mountains, that were thought to be fixed, 'flowing past like clouds', the geologist is able to see in this an anticipation of the theory of tectonic plates according to which 'the continents, with their mountains (to a depth of 100km from the surface of the Earth) move about like lumps of earth floating on a viscous asthenosphere, and can diverge, giving rise to a new ocean, or else converge, giving rise to mountains, or else float parallel to each other', p. 175.

155. *Reconstruction*, p. 60.

156. *Reconstruction*, p. 64. My emphasis of the word 'reconstruction'.

157. The *Kalâm*, literally the 'Word', refers to the discourse that proposes to use reason to support the truths of faith. In the second century of the Hijra appeared the *Kalâm of the Mu'tazilah* (also called 'the dissidents') who referred to themselves as the 'supporters of justice and unity': these rationalists professed, in effect, that affirming the justice of God in punishment and reward assumed that man was totally free in his acts; that his unity assumed he had no distinct features that coexisted, in some way, with his unique essence. In reaction against this current of thought, Abu Hassan al Ash'ari (died in 935) will give birth to a *Kalâm* that bears the name of *Ash'arism* which presented itself as a more moderate rationalism. This school, which will coexist with Mu'tazilism, created the cosmology, referred to here, of atoms and accidents continuously supported by the acting power of God who is thus, in fact, the only true agent, created being only 'borrowing' action.

158. *Reconstruction*, p. 169.

159. *Reconstruction*, p. 65.

160. 'Islam et la science', *Les religions d'Abraham et la science*, p. 135.

161. Cited by Homa Pakdaman, in *Djamal ed-Din Assad Abadi dit Afghani*, Paris: Maisonneuve et Larose, 1969:82.

162. Cited by Homa Pakdaman, in *Djamal ed-Din Assad Abadi dit Afghani*, p. 82.

163. These reactions which, for some, went so far as to raise doubts as to whether Al Afghânî was truly the author of this response, are analyzed by Pakdaman, *Djamal ed-Din Assad Abadi dit Afghani*, p. 82 onwards.

164. Cf. *Reconstruction*, pp. 135-136.

165. This article by Al Afghânî is reproduced pp. 101-122 in Nikki R. Keddie, *An Islamic Response to Imperialism: Political and Religious Writings of Sayyid Jamâl ad-Dîn 'al-Afghânî'*, Berkeley, Los Angeles, London: University of California Press, 1983; quote p. 122.

166. *Reconstruction*, p. 6.

167. *The Secrets of the Self*, song VII titled 'To the Effect that Plato, Whose Thought has Deeply Influenced the Mysticism and Literature of Islam, Followed the Sheep's Doctrine, and that We Must Be on Our Guard Against His Theories'. We can observe that in the 'reversal of Platonism', Muhammad Iqbal picks up Nietzschean threads and opposes the lions – tigers in the English translation to the sheep in these terms:
The wakeful tiger was lulled to Slumber by the sheep's charm.
He called his decline Moral Culture.
(*The Secrets of the Self*, song VI titled 'A Tale of which the Moral is that Negation of the Self is a Doctrine Invented by the Subject Races of Mankind in Order that by this Means They May Sap and Weaken the Character of Their Rulers', line 629-630.

168. *The Development of Metaphysics in Persia*, p. 38.

169. *Reconstruction*, p. 144.

170. *The Mysteries of Selflessness*, French ref. p. 130

171. *Reconstruction*, p. 144.

172. *Reconstruction*, p. 154.

173. *Reconstruction*, p. 120.

174. Muhammad Abduh, French: Rissâlat al Tawhîd / *Exposé de la religion musulmane*, p.108.

175. Cf. *Reconstruction*, p. 77.

176. On the points concerning inheritance and divorce, cf. *Reconstruction*, pp. 160-162. On these same questions and on polygamy, cf. *Writings and Letters*, pp. 63-67: this is the text of an interview granted by Iqbal to the *Liverpool Post* at the time of the round table. Iqbal declares there: 'Monogamy must be our ideal. But what remedy do we have when the number of women exceeds the number of men?', p. 66.

177. *Islam, l'autre visage*, p. 125.

178. Cf. Abu Nasr al Farâbi, *Book on Religion*.

179. In *Speeches and Statements of Iqbal*, pp. 109-139.

180. Cf. *Speeches and Statements of Iqbal*, pp. 130-134.

181. Michel Foucault, 'What is Enlightenment?' in *Ethics: Subjectivity and Truth. The Essential Works of Michel Foucault 1954-1984*, Volume One, trans. Robert Hurley et al (Allen Lane The Penguin Press, 1997), p. 309. This also means that if there is a movement of convergence of societies and cultures within an attitude of modernity, this doesn't indicate a cultural homogenisation. We can thus speak, with Charles Taylor, of 'alternative modernities'. On this point, we can read with interest the debate on alternative modernities initiated by the journal *Public Culture* (issue edited by Dilip Parameshwar Gaonkar *Alter/Native Modernities*, Vol. 11, no 1, Winter 1999), in particular the article by Charles Taylor – 'Two Theories of Modernity' – and that by Thomas McCarthy – 'On Reconciling Cosmopolitan Unity and National Diversity'.

182. On this level, he points out, it is the same as the case of slavery. In the limitations that were imposed on this practice and in the multiplicity of recommendations aiming to free slaves, we can clearly read the intention to abolish slavery which, today, simply forbids it.

183. Richard K. Khuri, *Freedom, Modernity and Islam: Toward a Creative Synthesis* (Syracuse: Syracuse University Press, 1998), p. 337. The emphasis in the text is the author's.

184. Amir Ali, pp. 183-184.

185. Amir Ali, pp. 183-184.

186. Amir Ali, p. 353.

187. *Reconstruction*, French ref. p. 108.

188. Jean-François Bayart, *The Illusion of Cultural Identity*, p. 235.

189. *Reconstruction*, p. 160.

190. *Reconstruction*, p. 165, p. 169.

191. *Reconstruction*, p. 155.

192. Ernst Troeltsch, *Protestantism and Progress. A Historical Study of the Relation of Protestantism to the Modern World*, trans. W. Montgomery, Boston: Beacon Press, 1958:64.

References*

Muhammad Iqbal's Works

Baal-i-Jibrül [Gabriel's Wing], English translation by Naeem Sidiqqi, (available online at the Iqbal Academy Pakistan site: http://www.allamaiqbal.com/).

L'Aile de Gabriel, French translation by Mirza Saïd-Uz-Zafar Chaghtaï and Suzanne Bussac, Paris: Albin Michel, 1977.

Le Message de l'Orient, French translation by Eva Meyerovitch with Mohammed Achena, Paris: Les Belles Lettres, 1956.

Les secrets du soi, followed by *Les mystères du Non-Moi*, French translation by Djamchid Mortazavi and Eva Meyerovitch, Paris: Albin Michel, 1989.

Letters and Writings of Iqbal, compiled and edited by B.A. Dar, Karachi: Iqbal Academy, 1967.

Letters of Iqbal to Jinnah, Lahore: 1963.

Message from the East, English translation by M. Hadi Hussain (available online at the Iqbal Academy Pakistan site: http://www.allamaiqbal.com/).

Reconstruire la pensée religieuse de l'islam, French translation by Eva Meyerovitch, Paris: Maisonneuve, 1955 *Javid Nama*, English translation by Arthur J. Arberry, (available online at the Iqbal Academy Pakistan site: http://www.allamaiqbal.com/).

Speeches and Statements of Iqbal, compiled by A. R. Tariq, Lahore, 1973.

The Development of Metaphysics in Persia: A Contribution to the History of Muslim Philosophy, London: Luzac and Company, 1908.

The Mysteries of Selflessness: A Philosophical Poem, English translation from the Persian by Arthur J. Arberry (available online at the Iqbal Academy Pakistan site: http://www.allamaiqbal.com/).

The Reconstruction of Religious Thought in Islam, London, Humphrey Milford: Oxford University Press, 1934.

The Secrets of the Self, English translation by Reynold A. Nicholson (available online at the Iqbal Academy Pakistan site: http://www.allamaiqbal.com/).

---

* When particular passages from a French translation, such as the introduction or any remark by the translator has been quoted in the book, the French translation is cited here in addition to the English version.

Other Works Cited

Abduh, Muhammad [Abdou, Mohamed], *Rissâlat al Tawhîd ou Exposé de la religion musulmane*, French translation by B. Michel and Cheikh Moustapha Abdel Razik, Paris: Librairie orientaliste Paul Geuthner, 1984.

Abdur Rahim, Khawaja, *Iqbal, the Poet of Tomorrow*, Lahore: Abdul Hameed Khan,1968.

Ali, Sayyid, Amir, *The Spirit of Islam: A History of the Evolution and Ideals of Islam with a Life of the Prophet*, London: Christophers, 1922.

Al-Ghazâlî, Abu Hamid, *The Incoherence of the Philosophers*, English translation by Michael E. Marmura, Provo: Brigham Young University Press, 1997.

Al-Farâbî, Abu Nasr, *The Book of Religion*, in *The Political Writings, «Selected Aphorisms» and Other Texts*, edited and translated by Charles E. Butterworth, Ithaca,NY: Cornell University Press, 2001.

Al Mujahid, Sharif, *Quaid-i-Azam Jinnah: Studies in Interpretation*, Karachi: Quaid-i-Azam Academy, 1981.

Anawati George C., Gardet, Louis, *Mystique musulmane. Aspects et tendances expériences et techniques*, Paris: Vrin, 1986 (4th ed).

Bayart, Jean-François, *The Illusion of Cultural Identity*, English translation by Steven Rendall, Janet Roitman, Cynthia Schoch, and Jonathan Derrick, Chicago: The University of Chicago Press, 2005.

Berger, Gaston, *Phénoménologie du temps et prospective*, Paris: Presses Universitaires de France, 1964.

Bergson, Henri, *Creative Evolution*, trans. into English by Arthur Mitchell, New York: Henry Holt and Company, 1911.

Bouamrane, Cheikh, Gardet, Louis, *Panorama de la pensée islamique*, Paris : Sindbad, 1984.

Cixous, Hélène, *L'Indiade ou l'Inde de leurs rêves*, Paris: Théâtre du Soleil, 1987.

Collective, *Les Religions d'Abraham et la science*, Paris : Maisonneuve et Larose, 1996.

Deleuze, Gilles, *Nietzsche and Philosophy*, translation by Hugh Tomlinson, London: Athlone Press, 1983.

Fakhry, Majid, *A History of Islamic Philosophy*, New York: Columbia University Press, 1970.

Foucault, Michel, 'What is Enlightenment?' in *Ethics: Subjectivity and Truth. The Essential Works of Michel Foucault 1954-1984*, Volume One, trans. Robert Hurley et al., Allen Lane, The Penguin Press, 1997.

Gaonkar, Dilip, (Editor), *Public Culture, Alter/Native Modernities*, Vol. 11, no 1, Winter 1999: Duke University Press.

Hallaj, Hussain Mansûr, al-, *Dîwân de Halladj*, French translation and presentation by Louis Massignon, Paris: Seuil, 1981.

Hussain, Riaz, *Towards Pakistan: The Politics of Iqbal*, Lahore: Islamic book service, 1977.

Kane, Cheikh Hamidou, *Ambiguous Adventure*, translation by Katherine Walker, New York: Walker and Company, 1963.

Keddie, Nikki, R., *An Islamic Response to Imperialism: Political and Religious Writings of Sayyid Jamâl ad-Dîn 'al- Afghânî'*, Berkeley, Los Angeles, London: University of California Press, 1983.

Khuri, Richard, *Freedom, Modernity and Islam. Toward a Creative Synthesis*, Syracuse: Syracuse University Press, 1998.

Maitre, Luce-Claude, *Mohammad Iqbal*, Paris: Seghers, 1964.

May, Lini, S., *Iqbal. His Life and Times*, Lahore: Ashraf, 1974.

Meyerovitch, Eva, *Islam, l'autre visage*, Paris: Albin Michel, 1991.

Morin, Edgar, *Amour poésie sagesse*, Paris: Seuil, 1997.

Nehru, Jawaharlal, *The Discovery of India*, New York:The John Day Company, 1946

Pakdaman, Homa, *Djamal ed-Din Assad Abadi dit Afghani*, Paris: Maisonneuve et Larose, 1969.

Qadir, Abdul, Sir, *Iqbal the Great Poet of Islam*, Lahore: Sang-e-Meel Publications, 1975.

Qureshi, Saleem M. M., *Jinnah and the Making of a Nation*, Karachi: Council for Pakistan Studies, 1969.

Raschid, M. S., *Iqbal's concept of God*, London and Boston: Kegan Paul International, 1981.

Renan, Ernest, *Averroès et l'averroïsme*, Paris: Maisonneuve et Larose, 1997.

Suhrawardî, Shihabuddîn, Y., *The Philosophy of Illumination*, English translation by John Walbridge and Hossein Ziai, Provo, UT: Brigham Young University Press, 2000.

Suhrawardî, Shihabuddîn, Y., *Le livre de la sagesse orientale*, French translation by Henry Corbin, Paris : Verdier, 1986. *The Philosophy of Illumination*, English translation by John Walbridge and Hossein Ziai, Provo, UT: Brigham Young University Press, 1999.

Teilhard de Chardin, Pierre, *The Divine Milieu*, translation by Sion Cowell, Sussex Academic Press, 2004.

Troeltsch, Ernst, *Protestantism and Progress. A Historical Study of the Relation of Protestantism to the Modern World*, trans. W. Montgomery, Boston: Beacon Press, 1958.